21 Rules
To Live By

21 Rules
To Live By
A Pathway to Personal Growth

River Publishing, LLC
Charleston, South Carolina

Published in the United States
by River Publishing LLC, Charleston, SC

© Steve Ferber 2012

First published September 2012

Library of Congress Control Number: 2012915728

ISBN #: 978-0-9852211-1-9

www.21rules.com
www.riverpublishing.net

Cover Design by Jay Deegan
www.deegancreative.com

Foreword

This book is perfect for my friend Mitch Williams who, so he tells me, often starts reading books in the middle. I don't quite understand how he does that. I've heard him explain it a dozen times: "Yes, I just open the book in the middle, and start reading."

Honestly, I don't get it, but in this case, with *21 Rules*, he'd be spot on, because this isn't one of those books that you read front to back. It's a skip-around book. Glance the contents, enjoy the poignant quotes on every page. Pick it up, put it down. Don't make it a chore. Reading shouldn't be a chore. Perhaps that's Rule 22.

Oh, and don't miss the Appendices, all 12 of them. They're chock full of great wisdom – none of it from me. I've simply gathered insight from world experts, and condensed it for you.

I've spent the better part of my adult life reading self-help books, and I finally realized that it was time to put my journalistic background to use. So this book, in essence, is a compilation of the wisdom shared over the years by self-help gurus. I've just brought it all together for you.

I'm happy to share some of my favorites (Rules 10 and 19 top the chart, along with Appendix F, titled "The Human Translator"), but you'll soon find some of your own, and I'd love to know what they are. So please send along an email (steve.ferber@gmail.com) to let me know. And don't be shy, I'd love to hear from you.

The inspiration behind this book, of course, are the four women with whom I'm madly in love – my wife Roe (this year, we celebrate our 35th year of marriage!) and our daughters Melyssa, Natalie and Olivia. Each of them is a gift from heaven, insightful, strong, in touch, motivated, caring, and wise. I love you.

(continued on next page)

And I love the friends and family who were kind enough to answer my endless series of questions, and who allowed me to publish their answers in this book (in special sections called, not surprisingly, "My Friends Share Their Thoughts"). Stop and read one or two, you'll be impressed with their insight.

So thank you to my sister Ilene, my sister-in-law Carole, uncle Allan, brother-in-law Bruce, cousins Chris, Jill, Marnie and Steeve (yes, it's two e's) and friends galore – Bobbi Cordingley, Carl Eckstein, Gail Chmura, Dave Rupp, Gary Miller, Joel Ann Rea, Joe Brancatelli, John Nelson, Jerry Semper, Kathy Dowd, Karin Udler, Marley Casagrande, Mickey Filipponi, Nat Emery, Ron Taylor, Sheila Filipponi, Vicki Hutman and Vicki Sullivan.

I'd also like to thank Jay Deegan, designer extraordinaire, who designed six versions of the book cover and impresses us daily with his genius. And finally, a special thank you to my good friend and colleague Elizabeth Bush who took the time to edit this book, and delight me with her comments, suggestions and critique. She is a special person. I wish each of you could meet her.

Thank you for picking this book up. I hope that it has meaning for you.

Steve Ferber
Charleston, South Carolina
September 2012

Contents

1   *Rules for Living Every Moment*

2   *Rules for Living With Yourself*

3   *Rules for Living with Others*

4   *Rules for Making Good Decisions*

5   *Rules for Achieving Your Goals*

6   *The Final Rule*

Appendices

My Friends Share Their Thoughts

Challenges

21 Rules
To Live By
A Pathway to Personal Growth

Introduction
The Window & The Wind

*"Man's greatness lies in
his power of thought."*
-- Blaise Pascal

In large measure this book is about our thoughts, the thoughts that our mind creates, and re-creates, as we experience life. Thoughts are said to be the window to our lives, but I believe that they are the wind as well.

There is no escaping the notion that our thoughts define our entire human experience -- they stand behind every word that we speak, every action that we take and (nearly) every emotion that we feel. Yet, knowing this, we spend but a fraction of our time examining our thoughts. Instead, we spend much of our day repeating tired and worn-out thought patterns.

*"The key to every man is
his thought . . . ."*
-- Ralph Waldo Emerson

This book is about changing those patterns, about thinking new thoughts, about capturing more happy moments, delivering more loving smiles. Central to our theme is the notion that we can *choose what to think*, that we actually have a *choice* about what private thoughts to ponder. But do we? Can we actually choose what to think?

Based on what we know about the physiology of the brain -- i.e., the neural competition between logic (the cerebral cortex) and emotion (the amygdala) -- it appears reasonable to speculate that:

1. We have some ability to choose what we think

(though our powerful emotional centers, honed over 40,000 years for survival, can easily overwhelm our logic systems);

2. Each individual's ability to "choose" varies dramatically, given that each human being is a unique blend of nature and nurture;

3. We all are capable of improving -- that is, each of us can enhance our ability to choose.

Do We Really Have a Choice?

As a youngster, then a teenager and young adult, I viewed choice as nothing more than "activity selection." In this context, choice meant deciding what to do next, with our personal and family time.

*"Every event that a man would master must be mounted on the run, and no man ever caught the reins of a thought except as it galloped past him."
-- Oliver Wendell Holmes*

"What book should I read next?"

"What restaurant should we go to for dinner?"

"What TV show should I watch?"

If we are fortunate, our lives offer many such choices. But the concept of choice goes far beyond mere activities -- choice encompasses all that we say (the words that we speak), all that we do (the actions we take), and, as I will soon argue, nearly all that we think (the thoughts that fill our minds).

Do We Choose What to Say?

Of course. After all, to avoid offending others with our words we can simply choose not to speak, (however difficult that may seem at times). Each day we're faced with thousands of decisions, none more critical than knowing when to speak and, in turn, knowing what to say. The words that we speak have enormous influence over our lives because they define the health of our relationships. This is why we must choose our words carefully, to make certain that we avoid, at all costs, speaking harshly to those whom we love.

Do We Choose What to Do?

No question. If we wanted to avoid offending others with our actions we can simply choose not to act -- to sit quietly and observe, and contemplate.

But Our Thoughts?

Can we really choose what to *think*? I believe that we can. I believe that it's possible to move our personal thought tracks ever so gently, in the direction that we desire. Granted, our thought patterns are deeply ingrained and may, indeed, solidify with age. But study after study, personal experience after personal experience, affirms that change is possible.

The key, of course, is awareness. After all, how can we change our patterns unless we know what they are?

"Life is the only game in which the object of the game is to learn the rules."
-- Ashleigh Brilliant

Hidden From the World

By and large, our mental habits are hidden from the world. That's why it's easier for a friend to tell us to stop smoking (physical habit), than to stop being self-critical (mental habit). Chances are that our friends probably know how many times a day we smoke a cigarette, but they likely have no idea how many times a day we privately criticize ourselves.

The world is obsessed with improving our physical habits -- we're told to eat a more nutritious breakfast, exercise three times a week, sleep a full eight hours a night. But where are the comparable preachings for improving our mental habits?

Yes, our mental habits may be hidden from the world, but they're certainly not hidden from us. The truth is, if you pause long enough to actually *watch* your thoughts, to observe and analyze them, you'll quickly notice how repetitive they are. Though each of us considers ourselves unique, and mysterious, and complex, the reality is that our thought patterns, our "private thought tracks," are quite predictable.

Rest assured, just as our neural networks instruct our body to move in a certain way (e.g., tying our shoelaces, swinging a golf club), these same neural networks instruct our mind to *think* in a certain way (e.g., getting upset when someone cuts us off in traffic).

"You become what you think about."
-- Earl Nightingale

Let's take an example. Say that a close friend tells you that you're being too sensitive. Chances are that the comment will trigger a sequence of familiar thoughts that lead you to criticize, both yourself and your friend. The patterns are all too familiar -- someone insults you and, in an instant, your cerebral CD begins playing "Thought Track #25."

Or, say that a person challenges your authority, In pops "Thought Track #41," triggering a well-worn sequence of anger and revenge. And so it goes, moment by moment, day after day, we play our pre-recorded thought tracks, over and over and over again.

It doesn't have to be that way. We can delete dislikable tracks and begin to re-stock the library. We can discard portions of our inventory and create fresh, new tracks for the coming season. Easy to do? Of course not, but the rewards are substantial. After all, aside from family and your friends, what's more precious than your private thought time?

Let's Get . . . Physical

I've often wondered why we spend so much time

trying to alter our physical habits (e.g., cutting down on food, alcohol or tobacco), but so little on our mental habits, why we spend so much time learning new physical skills (e.g., guitar, tennis, yoga, computer skills), but so little learning new mental skills. Perhaps it's because our physical habits are public, or perhaps it's because they're just easier to learn.

Perhaps. But imagine the benefits of learning new mental skills. Imagine building an internal system where thoughts create confidence and self-esteem.

Shouldn't we be paying more attention to our mental habits?

Creating Private Words of Encouragement

Words are among man's most powerful forces yet we often neglect to harness them. I'm sure that you can recall a moment in your life when a word or two -- from a person that you respect -- led you to change a personal decision, or perhaps, more dramatically, the course of your life. It may have been a simple suggestion (*"Why don't you give them a call?"*), or it may have been strong words of support (*"trust your instincts"*).

"Every thought we think is creating our future."
-- Louise L. Hay

I refer to these urgings as "public words of encouragement" because we take these public words and incorporate them into our private thoughts, to help us shape future decisions. We hear public words of encouragement not just from friends and relatives, but from authors and politicians, script writers and talk show hosts.*

---

* *I remember taking inspiration from a small mistake made by Helen Hunt at the Academy Awards presentation some years ago. She began by first mispronouncing, then missing entirely, a word or two. Five seconds into her presentation, she politely paused and said: "Let's start again." And so she did. No one criticized, no one blinked. Smoothly, and without fanfare, she simply decided to "start over," teaching us all how simple it can be, to begin again.*

Why not learn to create our own "private words of encouragement?" Why not start listening to ourselves? It is my fervent hope that *21 Rules To Live By* will help you do just that.

I recall how, standing at a funeral several years ago, I started to imagine what everyone was thinking. It seemed that, at this singular moment, all petty disputes had dissolved, all daily worries had diminished. During this one unique moment, it appeared that we were all of one mind -- sharing thoughts of love and warmth, of friendship and compassion. Yet, hours later, in the privacy of our car, or our home, or our thoughts, we quickly reverted to our hackneyed thought tracks, thoughts that criticize and condemn, destroy and diminish.

"Thought takes man out of servitude, into freedom."
-- Henry Wadsworth Longfellow

Now alone in the privacy of my car, I asked myself: since they're just *thoughts*, what prevents us from creating, and re-creating, the same thoughts that we experienced at the funeral? If they're just *thoughts*, what prevents us from creating them while we're sitting in traffic, weeding the garden, or paying the bills? Why must we revert to old patterns?

The answer, of course, is that we need not. All we need is a new set of tools.

In the physical world, we're presented with thousands of tools, each created and sold on the promise that they'll save you time or increase productivity. But rare are the tools designed to help us improve our mental outlook. Shouldn't we spend more time shopping for them?

Matching the Moments

21 Rules to Live By is one such tool, designed to relieve anxiety and tension, to diminish anger and aggravation, to redirect your thoughts to a happier, and healthier, place.

One of my primary goals in writing *21 Rules* was to make it practical, that is, to offer specific "words of encouragement" that you could share, with yourself, at just the right moment.

What moments are we talking about?

♦ moments when you're struggling with life's uncertainties (Rules 1-3);

♦ moments when you're overwhelmed with anxiety, trying to calm your nerves (Rules 4-8);

♦ moments when you're interacting with another person, be it a family member, a close friend, or a new acquaintance (Rules 9-13);

"The noblest pleasure is the joy of understanding."
-- Leonardo Da Vinci

♦ moments when you're trying to make a decision (Rules 14-17);

♦ moments when you're creating, then striving to reach, a personal goal (Rules 18-20); and

♦ moments when you're frustrated by people, or institutions, that remain unwilling to change (Rule 21).

In its simplest form, *21 Rules To Live By* is a "how-to" journal, offering specific words of encouragement for some of life's most anxiety-filled moments. Too often, after reading a self-help book, I was left wondering: "OK, I understand what the author is saying, *But, now, what do I do?* . . . to calm down, to feel better, to feel more relaxed?"

With this in mind, I crafted each of the 21 rules with specific moments in mind. The concept was, whenever one of these moments presented itself, there would be a rule -- a word of encouragement, of guidance -- to help bring us back to center, to ease the anxiety or the angst.

Example: when you're stuck in mind-numbing traffic and your temperature is starting to rise, turn to Rule 4 (Live in the Present) or Rule 5 (Focus on the Process). Or, perhaps you're privately negotiating a career change -- Rule 14 (Listen To Your Heart) can help.

Step #1

Mind you, the concept of linking words to moments may seem far too simplistic to generate meaningful, long-lasting, change. Consider then these rules, these words, as a first step towards building new thought habits, new ways of thinking about our day's travails. The truth is, while life is both dynamic and unpredictable, our thought tracks often are not, and the more quickly we recognize this, and take steps to change them, the happier we will be.

"It's only a thought, and a thought can be changed."

-- Louise May

On a personal note, I often have used these rules during times of stress and frustration, and, I am pleased to report, have experienced notable success. Naturally, I'm not always soothed by just words (intense moments seem to overwhelm my ability to listen). But, more than not, these private words have helped my mental outlook, releasing my private thoughts to travel in new directions. In essence, these rules have helped create more mental time, more time for me to dream and create, instead of grouse and complain.

My hope is that, as you read this book, you'll find a rule or two that works for you (naturally, more would be wonderful). My hope is that you'll find a rule that, when applied at just the right moment, brings you a sense of inner calm, or peace, and lasts for more than a moment. If that should be the case, I will be pleased beyond measure.

This book is not intended as a scientific journal

(though it's peppered with references), nor does it aim to explore the physiology of the human thought process (it does touch, briefly, on auditory and visual cues). Instead, this book is simply a bid to offer personal words of encouragement that you can share with yourself, as your moments unfold.

Why 21?

I selected "21" rules for a highly scientific reason: all three of our daughters (Melyssa, Natalie & Olivia), and now our first grandchild (Emery) are born on the 21st. My wife Roe delivered all three girls naturally, that is, no scheduled C-sections. My mother loved the coincidence of nature because it was easy for her to remember her granddaughters' birth dates -- she only needed to remember the month (September, February and March, by the way, just in case you're planning to buy a gift). Naturally, since the birth of our daughters, the number 21 has become something of a family emblem, not to mention that blackjack is my favorite card game.

"Thoughts have power, thoughts are energy. And you can make your world or break it by your own thinking."
-- Susan Taylor

Why *These* 21?

The process of selecting the 21 rules was, to be sure, a touch more scientific. It involved matching life's moments (e.g., alone with our thoughts, talking to others, making decisions, setting goals) with specific rules (it should be noted, however, that the list of 21 is not necessarily in order of importance; instead, they're grouped according to moments, to facilitate recall).

The ongoing debate within the family continues over Rule #1. For the better part of a decade Rule #1 was to "have fun" (it's still in the mix, don't worry). My wife Roe and I stressed this rule because, particularly on the athletic field, players often forgot to enjoy themselves. Instead, the athletic field became yet another battleground of ego and personality. Too often, young athletes were told to focus on winning,

---

Don't Miss These!

If you're tight for time, make sure you that don't miss these three passages (some of my favorites):
-- "You Don't Need More Self-Discipline" (page 68);
-- The Firm-Flex Continuum (Rule 19, page 169); and
-- Laughing All the Way (page 62).

"The Law of Attraction attracts to you everything you need, according to the nature of your thought life. Your environmental and financial condition are the perfect reflection of your habitual thinking. Thought rules the world."

-- Joseph Edward Murphy

instead of effort, to emphasize aggression instead of compassion (no wonder we struggle to build tolerance between races and nations). So "having fun" became a central family theme. The fact that it's been supplanted by a new #1 will likely stir family debates for the next decade, or two.

The Rules Themselves

Here then is a quick look at the 21 rules, grouped into six broad categories:

Rules for Living Every Moment

Rule #1: Be Kind to Yourself
Rule #2: Have Fun
Rule #3: Work Hard

As noted, for the better part of ten years our family's #1 rule was to have fun. In our current list, it hasn't fallen far (it's now #2), but that doesn't prevent our daughters from giving us grief, now and again. They insist that having fun is still #1 in their hearts. Far be it from us to disagree.

But the new #1 -- Be Kind to Yourself -- is a worthy competitor because of its power to transcend all others. Too often, we privately criticize ourselves, attacking both our decisions and behavior. By and large this self-criticism is detrimental to our well-being, blunting our ability to grow and evolve.

Rule #1 is a variant on the golden rule -- treat yourself as you wish for others to treat you, with kindness and patience, with grace and compassion. This isn't to say that self-criticism doesn't have its place -- it does, as guilt and self-examination are worthy assets on the road to self-discovery. But, too often, our private self-judgment serves to lessen, not lift up, our sense of self.

Rules for Living with Yourself

Rule #4: Live in the Present
Rule #5: Focus on the Process
Rule #6: Pause
Rule #7: Laugh
Rule #8: Create New Habits

Years ago I read the following quote: "Not one person in 10,000 can live in the present." The quote intrigued me and has generated years of self-thought about both the meaning of that phrase and the enormous challenge of doing so. Rules 4 and 5 urge us to focus on the moment, however impossible that may seem. And Rules 6, 7 and 8 offer us a pathway for *what to do* when confronted by anxiety and frustration.

"You are today where your thoughts have brought you; you will be tomorrow where your thoughts take you."
-- James Allen

Life presents no shortage of moments in which to employ these five rules, each aimed at helping us live with ourselves.

Rules for Living with Others

Rule #9: Respect PPIs (Personal Preference Items)
Rule #10: Avoid USSs (Unsolicited Suggestions)
Rule #11: Listen
Rule #12: Be Kind to Others
Rule #13: Help Others

Feel free to skip this section if you: 1. live alone; 2. never interact with other people; and 3. have no plans for engaging with others. For the rest of you, you'll probably enjoy Rules 9 and 10, which address respect and personal preferences.

This group of rules also includes one of my favorites: listen (#11). It's quite possible that listening is the *most important human skill that is never taught*. More about this later.

Rules for Making Good Decisions

Rule #14: Listen To Your Heart
Rule #15: Take Risks
Rule #16: You're Free To Change Your Mind
  At Any Time
Rule #17: Welcome Mistakes

"We find it hard to believe that other people's thoughts are as silly as our own, but they probably are."

-- James Robinson

Regardless of what kind of decision you're making, these four rules will easily apply. Rules 14 and 15 are designed to help you while you're making your decision, Rules 16 and 17 will guide you *after* you've made your decision. My favorite from this set is Rule 16 (You're Free to Change Your Mind At Any Time). It's one of the most popular rules in our house!

Rules for Achieving Your Goals

Rule #18: Zero to One
Rule #19: Be Firm, Yet Flexible
Rule #20: Set Goals, Not Expectations

If you're the kind of person who sets personal goals, you'll enjoy these three, plus a detailed introductory section which describes the six major tenets of goal-setting, drawn from the world's leading experts. Rules 18 and 20 are designed for use *before* you set your goals in stone. And then there's my personal favorite, Rule 19 (Be Firm, Yet Flexible), which I seem to use daily, both to guide my decisions and actions and re-establish balance in my life. Whatever you do, don't miss Rule 19.

The Final Rule

Rule #21: Question All Rules

Some years ago we taught our daughters an important life rule -- "Seek Forgiveness, Not Permission" -- on the condition that they would never use it against us. I still love that rule and use it frequently (as do our daughters) because it underscores the essence of Rule 21: Question All Rules.

Life is filled with a plethora of rules -- from grammar rules and union rules to driving rules and tax rules, just to name a few. I'm not a big fan of rules (making it all the more curious why I wrote a book entirely about rules), which is why I enjoy Rule 21.

Too often we are asked to follow rules of questionable logic (*"I'm sorry, sir, but that's just our policy"*), and soon our sense of fairness is piqued. I suppose that one could simply comply, and acquiesce, to the torrid stream of rules that run our lives. I prefer not. I assume the position that challenging rules is more than an option, it's an obligation, a responsibility. So as you read through these 21 offerings, please question them at will.

"All truly wise thoughts have been thought already thousands of times; but to make them truly ours, we must think them over again honestly, till they take root in our personal experience."
-- Johann Wolfgang Von Goethe

Goodness knows our daughters do.

Rules That Soothe

My hope is that, within these pages, you will find a rule or two that both suits and soothes. The truth is, we *can* re-write our personal scripts, we *can* think new thoughts, we *can* choose what we think.

So if you've ever been angry, frustrated, upset, overwhelmed, conflicted, worried, agitated, furious, frantic, uneasy, perturbed, anxious, nervous, tense, apprehensive, bored, annoyed, beleaguered or stressed . . . like me . . . then this book is for you.

Enjoy.

Sloppy Thinking
*"Sloppy thinking
gets worse over time."*
-- Jenny Holzer

Rule #1

Be Kind
To Yourself

"Accept everything about yourself -- I mean everything. You are you and that is the beginning and the end -- no apologies, no regrets."
-- Clark Moustakas

To begin, a short quiz.

Name the three people with whom you have spent the most time in the last two years. Feel free to place the book aside as you contemplate the answer. We'll wait. Hmmm, hmmm, hmmm.

No rush. Take your time.

Our quiz, of course, is a bit of tomfoolery but its answer is anything but. The person with whom you spend the *most* time, moment-in, moment-out (no need to jot this one down) is *you*. The point is translucent: when it comes to kindness we often neglect the person with whom we spend *all* of our time.

Why is that?

The world's universal message is to treat others kindly, to avoid criticism and blame, to impart love and understanding. We're encouraged to extend ourselves on all occasions, to bestow compassion and generosity

"It is of practical value to learn to like yourself. Since you must spend so much time with yourself, you might as well get some satisfaction out of the relationship."
-- Norman Vincent Peale

15

on our fellow travelers, in hopes that they will treat us in kind. So why, pray tell, do we abandon these precepts when dealing with ourselves?

You may have heard the popular maxim:

"The people we love the most are the ones we criticize the most harshly."

"Know that you are your greatest enemy, but also your greatest friend."
-- Jeremy Taylor

The adage reflects our paradoxical family life, but it also applies to our most intimate relationship, one which we often fail to cultivate and nurture. When was the last time you looked at yourself in the mirror and smiled? You smile at others, don't you? Why not smile at yourself? Why do we treat others more kindly than ourselves?

Rule #1 turns a centuries-old proverb into a modern-day adage:

Do unto yourself as you wish for others to do unto you.

We long for others to treat us gently, to forgive our missteps, to understand our failings and to shower us with love. If we ask this of others, why not ask it of ourselves?

"You yourself, as much as anybody in the entire universe, deserve your love and affection."
-- Buddha

Lest we relegate self-criticism to the back shelf, let's acknowledge that animadversion has its place, for a proper dose of introspection and self-critique often leads us to act responsibly. But, taken to extremes, self-criticism becomes a nagging, negative force which often chips away (sometimes, eats away) at our self-confidence and good nature.

Rule #1 carries a gentle message -- when dealing with *you*, be kind, tender, compassionate, patient, thoughtful, caring and loving. Rule #1 says to treat yourself as you would a close friend -- by listening with compassion, by accepting mistakes, by being a calm voice in a troubled sea and by using words that soothe (not criticize) when you're upset.

So be kind, to yourself. And remember that the person to whom you're directing this kindness will appreciate it. Guaranteed.

Challenge 1A
Treat Yourself

Why wait for your birthday? It seems fashionable, of late, to make gift lists for every occasion, not just birthdays. Why not create one of your own?

Gillian Butler & Tony Hope, authors of *"Managing Your Mind,"* maintain that "giving yourself treats is a skill that needs to be developed." The first step? "To give yourself permission to have treats." Butler & Hope explain: "Treats bring pleasure, and pleasure is worth having purely because it makes you feel good. But treating yourself will also enable you to accomplish more, and enable you to change in ways that are right for you."

They add: " . . . The wonderful thing about treats is that they can give pleasure well beyond what would seem possible. The secret is to choose the right treats for you. Once we are grown-up, life can become so full of chores, both at home and at work, that it is easy to get bogged down in routine and forget pleasure. . . . It is when life's problems are getting on top of you that it becomes particularly important to reward yourself . . . ."

Your Two-Step Challenge

Step 1. Make a list of things that you enjoy; and
Step 2. Refer to the list, as often as possible *(for examples, see Appendix A)*. And here are two hints, to guide you:

a) The longer the list the better; and
b) Remember to include treats both large (taking a vacation) and small (e.g., spending a few extra minutes over breakfast).

See Appendix A for ways to treat yourself (p189)

The Author's Friends Share Their Thoughts
In a bid to learn how others think, the author assembled a panel of 30 friends (psychologists and social workers among them) to answer some of life's most penetrating questions. Excerpts of their answers appear below.

The author asked his friends:
Do you treat yourself kindly?

"Don't you think [treating ourselves kindly] evolves with age (like all other good things!)? I truly believe that we gain so much wisdom through experience, and it becomes easier each day to practice what we preach, take one day at a time, view life as short, etc., etc. All those cliches that I heard as a child suddenly take on new meaning! My guess is that no one of us is as kind to ourselves as we are to others, although I'll bet (and hope) many of us are a lot kinder than we used to be." -- Marley C.

* * *

"I have known [how important it is to treat myself nicely], and have preached that to others, for years. Why is it that I have so much trouble doing it myself? The old saw is true: 'Physician, heal thyself.' [Treating oneself well is] something to work for instead of going complacently through life." -- Nat E.

* * *

"It's a tough question. . . . Lately there has been a lot of activity in our lives and we just aren't getting younger. I believe we are just as critical of ourselves as always. However, speaking for myself, I find myself realizing that I have done my best and letting myself get off a little easier than in my younger days. In the old days I would work until the job was finished in accordance with my own high personal standards. Today, I will push myself, however, when I start feeling the wear and tear I evaluate where I am and take the time to get the batteries recharged. Some old military expressions that describe this feeling are:

'Fought and lived to fight another day.
Discretion is the better part of valor.'

"So, in summary, I treat myself with a little more kindness so I can return and get back in the fray the next day. To revert back to the old days would be detrimental to one's health. Taking a time out isn't bad; it's sort of treating yourself to kindness. Perhaps it's a sign of old age, but I have learned to appreciate the simpler things of life such as: a dinner at home with all of the family members in attendance; attending church services as a family; dining in or dining out with some good friends; spending a day with some old friends to discuss life in general." -- Dave R.

Loving Yourself
"If you aren't good at loving yourself, you will have a difficult time loving anyone, since you'll resent the time and energy you give another person that you aren't even giving to yourself." -- Barbara De Angelis

Rule #2

Have Fun
Anytime, Anywhere

"Now and then it's good to pause in our pursuit
of happiness and just be happy."
                    -- Guillaume Apollinaire

Who decides when you're having fun?

The question brings to mind a memorable line from
The Four Seasons, a movie in which old friends bid
to re-connect. Following a tense moment of relational
friction, Carol Burnett turns to her friends and asks:
"Are we having fun yet?"

"Fun is a good thing,
but only when it spoils
nothing better."
-- George Santayana

The question, though playful, carries an answer of
considerable consequence, for how is it that we achieve
fun? Who decides when we're having it? And, more
importantly, how does one acquire it?

First and foremost, it's important to embrace the
notion that having fun is a skill, one that we can both
cultivate and nourish. Some, of course, believe that the
skill is innate, but I beg to differ. Having fun is no different than handwriting, web design, hopscotch or golf;
they're all worth developing (yes, even hopscotch).
But how?

Challenge #1: Where Does Fun Live?

Our first challenge is to find out where fun lives.
Based on life's unwritten rules, fun is reserved for

special places (e.g., beaches, theaters, golf courses, amusement parks and restaurants) and special occasions (e.g., weddings, birthday parties and vacations).

What does your fun profile look like? Where do you experience the most fun? Chances are that your fun profile will reveal consistent patterns, of people, places and activities. The trick, of course, is to find ways to expand your universe to new venues -- e.g., waiting in traffic, cleaning out the garage, paying the bills or doing homework.

Imagine, just for a moment, if you were capable of having fun anywhere, anytime, no matter the task.

You're laughing now, I can hear you. You're thinking: how absurd to think that fixing a flat, waiting in line or talking to a telemarketer at dinner time can be enjoyable. Perhaps. But if you take a moment to examine the concept, you'll soon see the possibilities.

Challenge #2: Who Decides When You're Having Fun?

Logic would dictate that you, and you alone, are in control, that you make the call. Don't be deceived. The external world -- the institutions that speak to us and the people who control them -- plays a major role in shaping our view of "fun." Case in point: Hollywood. And after a while, it's safe to assume that our internal thoughts begin to conform to these notions.

How then do we fight the wave? Here's one approach.

Step 1: Observe Your FZs

Begin by exploring your fun zones (FZs), that is, the activities and places that you associate with fun. The key is to observe your thought patterns because thoughts, not places, are what create the "fun" experience.

Step 2: Understand

It's important to remember that changing one's thought habits can be both difficult and frustrating, so patience is in order. The key to any personal change is observation, awareness and perspective. But it takes time. So be kind to yourself (Rule #1) and patient with your progress. Don't demand too much.

Step 3: The Grand Thought Experiment

Now the fun part -- the Grand Thought Experiment. The next time you're in a UFZ (Unauthorized Fun Zone), be it a fixed thought track or an undesirable place, try to move your thoughts, ever so gently, in a positive direction.

UFZs surround us. Each day we encounter traffic jams, hostile bosses, checkout lines, family conflicts, household chores, and disgruntled work associates. And, all too often, when we enter a UFZ, we trigger the same series of negative thoughts, negative impressions. In so doing, we miss an opportunity to re-program.

Here's one of my favorite examples.

It's moving day and you're thoroughly exhausted from weeks of preparation and transition. The moving crew is pulling out after four grueling hours of unloading. Boxes are everywhere. Stress level and personal fatigue have reached epic proportions.

The phone rings and your sister-in-law asks you how you're holding up. Moments later, you utter those unmistakable words -- "I can't wait until the boxes are unpacked."

"Even the worst of jobs has their pleasures; if I were a grave digger or a hangmen, there are some people I could work for with a great deal of enjoyment."
-- Douglas William Jerrold

The message, though subtle, is clear: when the boxes are away, when the kitchen drawers are lined, when the drapes are up, when the garage is organized, when the workbench is ready for use, THEN I'll be happy. And not a moment sooner.

The telltale phrase, of course, is "I can't wait until . . . ."

Waiting in an Illusion

Hard as we try to enjoy the moment, we're forever waiting to enjoy ourselves, waiting to have fun, waiting to complete the perceived drudgery to experience that "happy moment," somewhere down the line.

"People rarely succeed unless they have fun in what they are doing."
-- Dale Carnegie

Don't wait. Waiting is an illusion.

Imagine that you're on your way home, after a long day. Suddenly it's bumper to bumper traffic and that happy moment that you've dreamt about is slipping away. The point is transparent -- you're free to enjoy the moment at hand. There's no need to wait.

Or say you're home, anxious to curl up on the couch with a good book, when you remember the chores that await. So you think: "Ahhh, once those chores are finished, *then* I'll be happy."

Don't wait. Don't wait to be happy.

We spend an enormous part of our mental lives waiting to be happy, waiting for that happy moment. What's so strange is that many of these happy moments never materialize, and, when they do, they often disappoint. So don't wait.

Instead, start turning UFZs into FZs. And remember:

> ♦ It's possible to begin enjoying your new home from the moment you step inside;

> ♦ It's possible to enjoy mowing the lawn, fixing the shelf and repairing the leak in the faucet;

> ♦ It's possible to enjoy making a late-night run to the market, even if you're tired and cranky and are ready for bed;

> ♦ It's possible to enjoy preparing for a major presentation or going to your annual physical;

> ♦ It's possible to enjoy mulching the yard, however intent you might be on planting the new flowers; and

> ♦ It's possible to enjoy the writing process, even when you're endlessly stuck in mental traffic.

"The ultimate goal of a more effective and efficient life is to provide you with enough time to enjoy some of it."
-- Michael Leboeuf

So the next time you find yourself annoyed, frustrated, disappointed or disillusioned, think fun.

You can make it happen. Any time. Any place.

The Author's Friends Share Their Thoughts
In a bid to learn how others think, the author assembled a panel of 30 friends (psychologists and social workers among them) to answer some of life's most penetrating questions. Excerpts of their answers appear below.

The author asked his friends:
Is having fun a skill? If so, is it naturally acquired?

"I think it is a skill and I strongly suspect that it is naturally acquired by some and developed by others. Thinking about it in these terms for the first time, it seems and I sure do hope that by paying attention to one's patterns one surely [can] learn how to improve on their ability to have fun. Why wouldn't it be like other behavior modification?" -- Bruce J.

* * *

"It's not a skill, but more an intrinsic, naturally given ability that some are blessed [with]. Saying that, I do believe we are able to determine our destiny as to living/being in the 'time' of 'fun' or making that choice." -- Mickey F.

* * *

"I believe that one can learn to have fun/more fun if one can get in touch with internal barriers to such enjoyment. Sometimes it takes external help to identify/deal with the barriers." -- Allan H.

* * *

"I believe we all have the capacity for fun, but vary in our opportunity and ability (skill) to have fun. I think there are many ways to have fun and this varies from person to person. There is the fun that you have because you enjoy an activity and are so caught up in it you don't realize how much fun you are having. This has more to do with capacity and

opportunity. The other kind of fun is being able to enjoy what you have to do, and this, I think, can be more of an attitude or skill which can be developed over time. This is where I think your 21 rules start to come in, such as being mindful and being able to step back to see the absurd." -- Karin U.

* * *

"Having fun is a naturally acquired state one enters into. Fun is individual. People have fun in very different ways. Even the serious person may have fun being serious. Fun is dynamic, changing through life. Things one used to have fun doing may not be fun any more and other things are now fun. Once one has identified what is fun to them, one can improve their ability to increase the level or intensity of the fun they have (that part may be a skill) at an activity." -- Vicki H.

* * *

"Hmmm. Some folks do seem to have more facility for it or are more open to the experience. 'Fun' is in the eye of the beholder. Innately curious people and those who laugh often seem to find fun in many things. These are also often the people who are seldom bored, as their minds can be engaged by virtually anything. Does this mean they have a 'richer' brainscape? It would seem that you could shape fun skills by exposing those less adept to non-threatening fun environments and helping them give themselves permission to have more fun." -- Joel R.

The author asked his friends:
If having fun is a skill, what's your skill level?
And what was it 10 years ago?

"Skill assessment presently is 90%. Ten years ago, fun, at least for me, was more dependent on situations, company, demands of time, money availability and other external influences. I was more concerned with how to have fun, than what really was fun. Age has given me maybe a little insight and wisdom, and has made me appreciate that fun is a relatively simple concept. It does not require planning, money, success, demands, situations, or equipment. It requires only the desire to experience it." -- Kathy D.

* * *

"Part I: 70 (having fun is a high priority to me, this could explain why I have chosen to 'play' for a living!)

"Part II: 80 -90! Definitely it was higher 10 years ago. Why: More responsibilities, in both work and home life. Also less energy (no, I am not getting older!) to do the crazy fun thing I used to do, and to maintain the long hours doing fun things or squeezing in as much fun stuff as I could." -- Vicki H.

* * *

"If I am under low stress, I can have fun doing almost anything. Probably the same 10 years ago. If stress goes up, my ability to have fun diminishes." -- Carl E.

* * *

"Part 1: 25% skillful at having fun on every endeavor. I find it more difficult as I get older (why is that?). Youth is wasted on the young. Or is it that my memory is selective and I seem to only remember the fun in everything back when I was younger?

"Part II -- I would say that 10 years ago

my skill level was more at the 35% level." -- Mickey F.

* * *

"My skill level for having fun today is certainly higher than it was 10 years ago. But, I think this is like the water level in the river, it goes up and down, depending on 'the weather'. Some days, my skill level is really high. Others, it's much lower. (You'll notice I avoided the extended simile by avoiding the use of the term "drier".)

"On average, I gave myself less permission to have fun 10 years ago. Now, I sometimes look for Fun Zones by ordering dessert first.

"If I were to chart it, I'd say the skill of having fun is a line of ever increasing slope, like the Dow-Jones averages. It is not quantifiable, as in setting a specific value. ('All six year olds need to reach a 17.') It is relative. The same scene, the same 'fun' experienced by two individuals will bring about two different readings on 'the fun scale.' In childhood, fun is a function of social setting and feeling secure. A toddler's squeals will turn to howls in the presence of a stranger. At puberty, the slope increases again with some very high spikes. . . . Then, upon 'job acquisition,' the slope levels out again, but still increases. (Note: Job acquisition follows fraternity/sorority years, the last serious spikes for most of us.) Middle age brings more ups and more downs. (Menopause can go either way, depending on your point of view!) Finally, maturity settles in. This is when you are secure enough to have fun whenever you feel like it. . . . Final word: the only thing that prevents us from having fun is the weight of the bag of 'shoulds' we carry on our shoulders. -- Nat E.

The author asked his friends:
Who decides when you're having fun?

"This is a difficult question to ponder. Fun as an individual would mean the individual would be the only one who could decide if he/she is having 'fun.'

". . . Also, does society dictate what is 'fun' and not fun? Some societies find fun in things we would find alarming and dangerous whereas, what we deem as fun they might find strange." -- Mickey F.

* * *

"Is having fun -- enjoying myself? I can truly enjoy what I am observing in others -- students in a classroom, people helping each other, a great soccer, basketball or baseball moment, etc. I am having fun at these moments and all I'm doing is observing others.

"Soooooo, whenever I might say 'I enjoyed that,' I guess I am having fun and determining it myself. When I am with others and everyone is laughing and being fresh to each other, others may think I am having fun, because I am relaxing and showing a side of me that I don't often have time to 'let out.' I am probably NOT enjoying those moments, but others perceive me as having fun!! Go figure! I do have fun teasing others, so when I am in the company of my brother, my baby sister, my students or you, I really have fun!!" -- Gail C.

* * *

"It depends. Sometimes I decide in the midst of something that it is really fun; sometimes the anticipation of an activity by the group [I'm with] foreshadows an event as fun.

"There certainly are beliefs by society at large as to what is fun. For example, take the beach. If you tell just about anyone that you are going to the beach, their eyes will light up and they will think you're lucky to be going to the beach to have 'fun.' You might not be very excited in some cases, like if you are going with people you don't want to be with, or if you're going to a beach that you don't particularly like.

"Hopefully, you'll have more control over your life than this, or you'll be able to go again soon under more pleasant circumstances. Lots of factors go into 'fun,' and I agree that fun is often defined by society. Unless, of course, a person is brutally honest and admits that he/she doesn't expect to have fun. But in my experience, most people like to portray their spare time as filled with fun." -- Marley C.

* * *

"How can the decision of whether or not one is having fun exist with anyone but the individual . . . .in designing your own environment . . . even cleaning the house can be fun! REALLY . . . it just depends on how you go about looking at your environment. If you constantly perceive life as a series of challenges with no opportunity for enjoyment, then fun is not going to be an ingredient of every day life. Fun is what one makes of a situation." -- Kathy D.

* * *

"I decide when I am not having fun. It usually isn't until later that I realize that I had a good time. If I'm talking with intelligent people, I am usually having fun." -- Carl E.

The author asked his friends:

What prevents us from having fun?

"I am prevented from having fun when I have too many things to do. I love it when the kids tell me to 'lighten up' or 'chill.' My aunt always used to say, 'Don't worry about the dirt in the house. It will be there in 20 years. Take time to enjoy your children.' I need to remember that more often in regards to lots of things." -- Gail C.

* * *

"I wish I knew. There in lies the crux of truly being 'happy' in one's life. It's not that I'm unhappy doing mundane chores. In fact I sort of get a bit of pleasure with them because they keep my mind off of other things. It's getting to them that sometimes is the 'test.' Becasue we do not like necessarily the 'thought of' doing these chores/tasks, we tend to put them off, but once we're into them and accomplish them, I find myself feeling 'good' about acheiving the task or getting it over with. And there are so many of these little silly tasks/jobs/things that we put off . . . cleaning the gas grill, painting the trim, cutting the grass, etc." -- Mickey F.

* * *

"The baggage we carry prevents us from, or allows us to, have fun. Exhaustion, hunger, poverty, weather conditions, etc., can prevent us from having fun. . . . " -- Marley C.

* * *

"A private was cleaning the floor around a conference table as three officers discussed sex. The Captain said, 'I think sex is 90% pleasure and 10% work.' The Major said, 'I think sex is 50% pleasure and 50% work.' And the General suggested that, 'Sex is 90% work and 10% pleasure.' Unable to agree, they turned to the private and asked his view. Replied the private, 'If there were any work in it at all, you'd have me doing it for you.' Whatever it is you would not want the private to do for you, has to be a plus on the fun side." -- Carl E.

The author asked his friends:

Where does fun live?

"Fun lives everywhere, except Kosovo. Wherever people can reflect and laugh at themselves or life's absurdities, you have fun. If it hurts, it ain't fun. Patch Adams had the knack for conversion." -- Carl E.

* * *

"Fun lives everywhere/anywhere. Fun is what one makes it to be. . . . It is enjoyment of life, and one's participation in life. Fun cannot be observed, it must be experienced. . . . It is the ability to appreciate the fact that we are alive and we can make choices. Fun is what it is made to be." -- Kathy D.

* * *

"That really depends on who you talk to, and when. Fun for me can be in my house in front of the fire with a book and some time. I LOVE THAT!! I know people who can't stand to be alone without one plan after another. Fun lives in the eyes of the beholder." -- Marley C.

* * *

"A quick thought on fun . . . I try to have fun with whatever I do, but I insist on having fun with any leisure time activities, or to further define it, non-work or responsibility related. If I am volunteering, doing cross-stitch, or reading a book, I want it to be fun. But I don't necessarily define fun as the laughing, squealing kind of activity; [instead,] I define it as something that gives me pleasure. And I'll try to find pleasure in the mundane, either by losing myself in my thoughts (which are probably 70% present; 30% past) or appreciating the simple act of accomplishment.

"My friends and family always grumble because I insist on frequently using my good, bone china dinnerware and sterling. They object because it must be washed and dried by hand. I have always said that I get as much pleasure from the simple act of washing and drying it as I do from using it. It's beautiful, I love it and I would rather wash and dry it than let it sit, unused and unappreciated, in a closed china cabinet. Maybe this isn't everyone's idea of fun but it floats my boat." -- Vicki S.

* * *

"Jollity: It's a frame of mind. Some people have fun doing the most ridiculous things. And no one else seems to have the same amount of fun, unless they are doing 'it' with the first person." -- Nat E.

Rule #3
Work Hard

"When I was a young man I observed that nine out of ten things I did were failures. I didn't want to be a failure, so I did ten times more work."
                    -- George Bernard Shaw

Chances are, if I had composed a list of rules a decade ago, "work hard" might not have cracked the top 20, no less the top 5. But with each passing day, with each new life experience, it's clear that *working hard* is the key -- to nearly everything. Whether you're building a relationship or building a reputation, working hard is the one ingredient you can't afford to leave out.

Not that we stop searching for alternatives. Let's be honest, we're forever looking for shortcuts, ways to reach our goals in less time, with less effort. But, as time and experience teach us, there truly *is* no such thing as a free lunch.

"Laziness may appear attractive but work gives satisfaction."
-- Anne Frank

Not to say that certain shortcuts don't deliver -- ATMs free us from long bank lines and computers free us from retyping our manuscripts on typewriters . . . and we certainly enjoy remote controls, ice makers, fast tolls, electric can openers and e-mail -- each designed to save us precious moments.

But to accomplish *goals of substance*, to develop relationships that last, there *are* no shortcuts. Still, we pursue them, affirming that we do, indeed, believe in magic.

If you watch television long enough, or read the day's news, or watch the frenzied pace in the corporate world, it's hard not to believe that life's penultimate goals are productivity and efficiency. The world's marketing engines drill the message home every day -- if you buy this new software package, this new cutting appliance, this new 3:1 drill kit, then you'll not only save time but you'll be more productive. The message gets stuck in our psyche and, after hearing the message for, say, the zillionth time, we actually begin to believe it.

"No one can arrive from being talented alone. God gives talent; work transforms talent into genius."

-- Anna Pavlova

Turn the Tide: Take the Long Cut

We spend exorbitant amounts of time pursuing shortcuts to manage our tasks. Fight back. Faced with a choice, try the long cut -- when you're slicing onions, try using the knife in place of the electric slicer. However appealing your shortcuts may be, a few milliseconds here and there won't earn you much. The truth is, shortcuts are one of life's most visible illusions.

"Successful people are not gifted; they just work hard, then succeed on purpose."

-- G.K. Nielson

For years I dreamed of having a beautiful garden, where flowers bloomed each month as the seasons passed. I chose the shortcut -- I bought a few perennials, installed an underground watering system and waited for the flowers to appear. Silly me, thinking that a garden would grow by itself. Now, each day that I work in the garden, I recall these simple words:

> *If you want to have a garden,*
> *you have to have a gardener.*

In other words, if you want to create products of substance, you have to do the work. No shortcuts, no end-arounds, no magic.

Attention All Mountain Climbers

When it comes to working hard, I often recall a

phrase composed by our daughter Natalie, some years ago. She wrote: "You have to climb the mountains before you can walk the plains." So, strap on your boots, and remember:

♦ When you and your spouse are clashing over money, *work hard* to understand your spouse's point of view;

♦ When you and your child are struggling over homework and curfews, *work hard* to understand how they feel, and why they struggle;

♦ When you're preparing a presentation, or cleaning out memorabilia that has been sealed for years, *work hard* to overcome the mental hurdles. Remind yourself that the harder you work, the more you will grow;

♦ When your boss is being unreasonable, the basement needs a new paint job, the new business isn't taking off the way that you had hoped, or the the car breaks down, again,

"If the power to do hard work is not a skill, it's the best possible substitute for it."
-- James A. Garfield

Work Hard

Don't shy away, don't withdraw, don't withhold your best for fear of failing. Simply work hard, and know that the skill you're improving is one of life's most precious treasures.

Rule 3 brings to mind a classic line delivered by Tom Cruise in the 1983 movie *Risky Business*. Commenting on his awe-inspiring vehicle, Cruise said, "Porsche, there's no substitute."

So it is with hard work. There *is* no substitute.

The Author's Friends Share Their Thoughts
In a bid to learn how others think, the author assembled a panel of 30 friends (psychologists and social workers among them) to answer some of life's most penetrating questions. Excerpts of their answers appear below.

The author asked his friends:
How important is it, in life, to work hard?

"This is one of my all-time favorite questions. I bet that our life here on earth will be ultimately judged not by how successful we were compared to others, but how well we used the tools (talents and abilities) God gave us.

"Everyone is different and that's what makes the world an interesting place. Just stand on a busy street corner, sit in a chair at the mall, eat a meal in a crowded cafeteria, sit in the stands at a professional or high school sporting event, or my favorite place to watch people was down on the infield of a horse racing track in New York. Or, better yet, watch people at the beach. . . .

"I imagine the second question when we approach the pearly gates will be: 'How well did we share the talents and gifts we had with others less fortunate?' Did we show genuine concern for others? Another question would be, 'How well did we train (mentor) younger generations with regards to using their talents and being concerned for others?' " -- Dave R.

* * *

"My personal learned experience is that to begin to get good at anything in my life has required hard work and dedication. It's true whether vocational, avocational, spiritual, relationship-based or just about anything else I can think of.

"As an additional observation, those who admire the achievements of others, frequently over estimate the value of someone else's 'natural ability' and underestimate the work they put in to excel." -- Bruce J.

* * *

"I think that it's terribly important to 'work hard' and I think that many of the feelings that people have of their life being 'successful' come from the sense of accomplishment that results of hard work.

"For me, my feelings about who I am as a person are strongly tied up with 'what I have accomplished', and what I have accomplished is usually directly tied up with the work I put into projects.

"I think that an important question related to this is how to balance 'hard work' against the rest of what life has to offer so that the work does not become an overriding consuming passion." -- Ilene F.

* * *

"In my experience, it is critical to work hard in life. Only then, when we have invested ourselves, do we celebrate our success. Things that come easily are not celebrated in the same way; we often wonder why they even happened. I guess it's the old external vs. internal locus of control. Did I do well on the test because I studied or because I lucked out

How important is it, in life, to work hard? *(continued)*

and it was easy?

"We take pride in what we work hard at. We reflect as we are working and probably revise, recharge, and forge ahead. We all need a payoff for hard work; when we get it (tangible or intangible), we feel successful.

"I associate the phrase with all aspects of life -- not just 'work' in the classic sense. Naturally, we associate 'working hard' with 'work,' that is, our daytime activities. But, certainly, we 'work' all the time -- to take care of our friends and our family, to meet obligations that come with being a responsible member of the human race. Thus, my interest in the term 'working hard' has as much to do with what we do at night, and on the weekends, as during the day." -- Marley C.

* * *

"One way to measure work is ergonomically. (An erg is a unit of work done by one dyne through a distance of one centimeter. A dyne is the amount of force that causes a mass of one gram to accelerate at the rate of one centimeter per second per second.) None of that is relevant except to say, we can measure work.

"If you accept that premise, perhaps you will accept that work is akin to effort. And there are many reasons to expend effort. It may be for remuneration, or for recreation. The reason we expend effort may be to please others, or to please ourselves. Or it may be for some unseen but anticipated future reward. At any rate, I think there is a reward in there someplace. Else, why expend the effort?

"How important is it to work hard? It depends on one's point of view. It may have a lot to do with the lens through which one views the world. Or, it may have to do with one's mood at the moment. There weretimes in my life when it also had to do with how much skill I had. . . .

"I suspect that 'working at something' has to do with reward. We will obviously work at things that will have direct impact. For example, the sailor on a sinking boat will work hard at bailing.

"But for other things, I think one's willingness to work hard is related to their ability to either make a connection to self ('It's important to me'), or to make a connection to someone or something that is important ('It's important to ___ that I make the effort'). There is some sort of payoff.

"I do think there are those who 'work hard' seemingly for others. There is no direct payoff for them. They appear to be doing things for others. My theory above begins to dissolve here and I don't have an explanation.

"Well . . . , I have progressed from Physics to Philosophy, all in about 350 words. It's time phor me to end this phoolishness and get some work done! Because it is personally satisfying. . . . And I want to get paid!" -- Nat E.

* * *

"It is paramount. I am surrounded by successful people who have sold their companies or retired. They crave work. The desire to apply oneself in a productive endeavor seems to have a biological driver. It appears to be more than a mere desire to be needed." -- Carl E.

* * *

"You have hit on a nerve (at least in my case). Growing up as I did in a true 'blue

Q: How important is it, in life, to work hard? *(continued)*

collar' home, we were taught (what seems in recollection) from the crib, that 'working hard will get you everything you want in life' or 'working hard is the only way to succeed.' And oh so many other idioms.

"Funny how the word 'ability' was seldom if ever used (at least in our household) in relation to discussion about 'work' or 'working hard.' Yet, in looking back, working hard was helpful in many, many instances where we were lucky enough to succeed in school, our jobs, our relationships, and in even life in general.

"But is it just as critical to have been blessed with the 'ability' to (a) make correct decisions, (b) to rationalize and decipher information, (c) to learn or grow from our education & even our life's experiences, (d) to retain and remember information, (e) to be able to communicate well and at the same time perhaps even more ciritically 'listen well,' (f) to have fun (yes I believe some are more blessed 'with the ability to do just that -- 'have fun,' whereas some of us just seem to lose this 'ability' somewhere on the road to life).

"See, I told you it hit a hot spot. May I go on? Is it 'fate' or 'karma' or just plain 'luck' when one becomes successful or was it a product of 'hard work?' Or was it, as I tend to believe, a rare combination of both one's fate combined with their 'ability' and 'hard work' that delivered such success? Are we not all to a great degree a 'product of our environment and educational process?' And I mean 'environment' more from the [perspective] of 'family'

first and then to 'peers and schooling.'

"Why is it that, more often than not, a family will have either parent (or parents) being doctors and then their subsequent children and children's children, become doctors down the line? It has to be more than 'ability' and 'hard work.' No?

"I once read an article about a couple [who] adopted two infants from a inner city mother. . . . This couple was . . . able to move to a remote area out west and, as I recall, raise their two infant sons in an area where they literally had to 'home school' them until it was time for University. [The kids took] their SATs, scored extremely high and were accepted to Yale & Princeton.

"Guess what happened? Both boys, while doing extremely well initially in college, eventually developed problems with their social skills [and] had difficulty later in their University years. Eventually, they graduated and went on in life, but not without a tremendous amount of 'hard work' at learning certain 'skills' we often take for granted growing up.

"Were these two brilliant minds? No doubt! However their 'ability' to communicate was found lacking. . . . They both had to 'work hard' to learn this 'ability.' Both, as I recall, went on to become well adjusted and [achieved some measure] of success. However my point here is that 'ability' is not always a substitue for 'hard work' or 'life in general,' but is [a critical factor] in gaining success in our endeavors." - Mickey F.

Rule #4

Live in the Present

"Learn from the past, set vivid, detailed goals
for the future, and live in the only moment
of time over which you have any control: now."
-- Denis Waitley

Day to day, where do you spend most of your time?

In the past? The present? Or the future?

On any given day, in any given moment, our private thoughts flow swiftly from the past to the present to the future -- a harsh word from yesterday (past) is mentally brushed aside as we listen to a colleague (present), then wonder about whether it might rain at the picnic on Sunday (future).

"You must live in the present, launch yourself on every wave, find your eternity in each moment."
-- Henry David Thoreau

Mental fitness experts laud the "present" and urge us to focus our energies on the moment -- on the person with whom we're conversing, on the task we're striving to accomplish, on the skill we're attempting to improve, on the decision that we're about to make.

The message is simple: the more focused we are on the present, the more fulfilling life will be. Instinctively, we know that this is true because of how good it feels to be fully engaged in the moment -- not brooding about yesterday or worrying about tomorrow.

What Exactly *Is* The Present?

Staying in the present, mind you, isn't to be confused with talking about the present. Imagine what a daunting task *that* would be! Let's be honest, a healthy chunk of human conversation involves sharing information about the past (*"What have you been up to?"*, *"How was your vacation?"*) or the future (*"We're going to a concert next week"* or *"Tomorrow, I plan to start looking for a new job"*).

By contrast, staying in the present . . .

. . . means focusing one's private thoughts on the moment, on the person or activity in front of you;

"Yesterday is a canceled check; tomorrow is a promissory note; today is the only cash you have; so spend it wisely."

-- Kay Lyons

. . . means listening to your friend share their daily struggles or your spouse share her worries about the future;

. . . means concentrating your energy on preparing the report, fixing dinner, listening to your client.

Our ability to stay in the present, of course, is perpetually at risk. And the most challenging moments are those when we're alone. When our thoughts start to drift, we risk missing the spendlor of the fruit on aisle 3, the shape of a clipped branch, the beautifully turned phrase, the magnificent contour of the green on the 17th hole.

Often, when I'm driving, I glance at the highest branch on a tree, and my daughter Melyssa says she too has adopted the habit. The idea, suggested in a passage I read some time ago (I can't recall the author), forces us to look outside of our daily frame, to see anew what this moment holds.

Melyssa and I often wonder how such a simple change can have such a dramatic effect. The skyward gaze always reminds me of a prophetic moment in the *"Dead Poets Society,"* when Robin Williams encourages his students to stand on their desks to alter their static view of the world.

Minimizing Thought Drift

Living in the present means attending to the task at hand, to the person or activity before you. It means minimizing thought drift in order to take full pleasure in all that lies before you. Let's be honest, when your mind drifts to that awkward social encounter, don't you lose your ability to enjoy this current moment?

We are thoughtful creatures, alternatively worrying, judging, imagining, justifying, evaluating, planning, fantasizing, problem-solving, lamenting, creating and scrutinizing. In the mixing bowl of thoughts, it's a wonder that we can keep our attention focused on *any* single task, for any meaningful length of time. Yet attention is key in our quest for fulfillment and life satisfaction.

"Finish each day before you begin the next, and interpose a solid wall of sleep between the two. This you cannot do without temperance."
-- Ralph Waldo Emerson

Each of us learns, at our own pace, that the more time we invest in the present -- the more time we spend looking at faces, and flowers -- the richer our lives become.

It seems trite to say, but we live life in the present. Certainly, we learn from the past and yes, it seems prudent to plan for the future. But in the final analysis, our life journey is composed of a continuous string of "presents," and when our thoughts drift ahead, or back, we lose a precious piece (or peace) of life's puzzle.

It's been said that one in 10,000 can consistently stay in the present.

May you be the one.

Challenge 4A
Use ESP . . . to take you back to the present

When your thoughts begin to drift, in ways that you define as unhealthy, try these three simple steps:

Step #1: Examine the Thought **(E)**
Ask yourself: am I drifting to the past or the future?

Step #2: Stop the Thought **(S)**
Make a conscious decision to stop the thought sequence;

Step #3: Return to the Person or Task **(P)**
Make a conscious decision to refocus your thoughts on the person with whom you're talking, on the activity in which you are currently engaged.

Caution: When employing E-S-P, please don't expect quick results. Chances are that the thought sequence you momentarily dismissed will soon reappear, cycling back into your conscious thought pattern. Don't despair. Simply observe how often, and with what intensity, it returns (it's reasonable to imagine that our thoughts have a half-life -- much like nature's chemical compounds -- and that their persistence is linked to their emotional charge; thus, as time goes on, the charge lessens and the thought sequence, once omnipotent, begins to weaken).

The key to E-S-P? Awareness and desire -- that is, becoming more aware of your thought patterns and exhibiting a desire to alter them.

Plagued by thought drift? Try E-S-P. Alternatively, take meaning from this brilliant quote, one housed on my friend's answering machine (thanks Jerry):

"The Past is History,
The Future is a Mystery,
This Moment is a Gift,
That is why we call it the Present."

The Author's Friends Share Their Thoughts
In a bid to learn how others think, the author assembled a panel of 30 friends (psychologists and social workers among them) to answer some of life's most penetrating questions. Excerpts of their answers appear below.

The author asked his friends:

How much time do you spend in the present vs. the past vs. the future?

"85% present, with lots of past and fast forwarding, and the 'present' as the pause button in between." -- Joel R.

* * *

"45% Present, 10% Past, 45% Future. To me, tomorrow is really the present, it's what I am always preparing for. So my present is really my future, too?? As soon as you are aware of the present, it's no longer the present, it's the past and you are in the future relative to it." -- Gail C.

* * *

"Past 10% (not worth much thought, move on, experience more!) . . . Present 50% (can be great, good, neutral, and terrible, either way you are stuck with it.) Present is what one has at hand that cannot be changed readily, ie. the job you have, the significant other, the house that needs painting, ...all those things one planned for (or didn't) when it "was" the future. . . . Future 40% (thinking of the future is how I keep my sanity! The future is how I dream it up, the way I want it to be.)" -- Vicki H.

* * *

"Present: 30% Past: 20% Future: 50%. The present is what you are experiencing at that moment. Your surroundings, who you're with and what you're thinking." -- Chris W.

* * *

"Present 50%, Past 35%, Future 15%. Can't define the present in PTT, because your PTs can sometimes be so overwhelming that you think you have been thinking for hours and it's just been minutes and you've traveled all over the place in your mind. You've been in the past, present and future of your mind in that time period." -- Carole E.

* * *

"20% Past, 40% Present, 40% Future (does this mean I am an optimist?) What one is thinking about in the past is important -- is it pleasantly reliving the past, or ruminating about mistakes or unpleasant events? I tend to connect the present to what might be ahead." -- Marley C.

How often do you say: "I can't wait until . . ."

"Always. Sometimes the anticipation is greater than the realization of something and doing the 'I can't wait . . .' aids in imagining what that something might look like, how it will go, what the end result might be. It also gives me a great lift to an ordinary, mundane, 'consistent' day." -- Carole E.

* * *

"Not often . . . 'I can't wait' suggests that all enjoyment, success, fulfillment, etc. looms somewhere over the horizon. I like NOW.

"The whole concept of 'I can't wait' to me suggests 'time freeze.' If we live continually in a state of anticipation we fail to notice the events of the moment. Since there is never a guarantee of happiness or success or fun or anything else in the future (life is too serendipitous for that), then living in a state of perpetual anticipation precludes having the opportunity to enjoy the present. Looking backwards to determine whether or not you have had fun may offer a clear view of the event, but the internal enjoyment of the moment is overshadowed by 'things yet to come' . . . the anticipation of 'having fun' cannot compare the actuality of it." -- Kathy D.

* * *

"Whenever I have an 'I can't wait until . . . ' moment, I immediately ruin it with the negatives that tag along: I can't wait to go to San Diego for 8 days. Will the dog be OK in the care of the kids? Will I be stressed from relaxing?, etc." -- Gail C.

Where do you spend your mental time?

"Human moments: I spend about 10% of my time musing, 20% thinking, 20 % conversing (more during the school year), 20% listening (40% interacting, which is a combination of conversing and listening), and 30% sleeping or being mindless. Dreams overlap with the other categories.

"I had a debate with a student last week about whether or not the brain can do more than one thing at a time. We agreed that the brain can stimulate more than one activity at a time -- seeing, hearing, tasting, talking, etc. all at one time -- but the brain can only be aware of one at a time." -- Gail C.

* * *

"Human Moments (not like a senior moment, right?). Musing: 5%, conversing: 40%, thinking: 30%, listening: 30%, interacting: 40%, acting (as in drama): 25% of the 40% conversing and the 40% interacting. At least that much of that time is acting when I am biting my tongue not to tell someone (usually a client) exactly what I think of what they just said, did, or what I think of their level of intelligence! The rest of the time is the real me.

"I definitely prefer listening, thinking, observing over interacting with most people . . . acting, as in physically doing something: 50% to 60% . . . . This answer could go on forever the more I think about it -- so I will spare you." -- Vicki H.

* * *

"Hard to put numbers to your categories without lots of thought, but I'll give a first guesstimate: musing: 4%, conversing: 12%, thinking: 20%, listening: 16%, interacting: 20%, sleeping: 28%." -- Allan H.

Rule #5

Focus on the Process
Not the product

> *"Take care of your minutes, and the hours
> will take care of themselves."*
> *-- Lord Chesterfield*

It may seem hard to believe, but every moment of our lives -- *yes, every moment* -- is a confrontation between *product* and *process*. Whether you're preparing dinner or a business plan, planning a wedding or a corporate takeover, leading a neighborhood food drive or a campaign against teenage drinking, it's *all* about *product* vs. *process*.

The *product* is the *end*, the final step. The *process* is the means, the road that leads us home.

Take food shopping. The *product* is that glorious moment when the bags are unpacked and the groceries are neatly tucked away. By contrast, the *process* is ongoing, and entails creating the shopping list, grabbing the reusable bags, driving to the supermarket, weighing the fruit, comparing cereal prices, chatting on the checkout line, leafing through magazines, paying the bill, carting the groceries . . . OK, you get the picture.

> *"The good life is a process, not a state of being. It is a direction, not a destination."*
> *-- Carl Rogers*

The point is, while we naturally strive to achieve the *product* (bags unpacked, goods neatly stored away), we sometimes become so fixated on reaching it that we fail to enjoy the *process*. In so doing, we miss countless opportunities to enjoy each step of the journey.

41

But we have a choice. Though it may not be readily apparent, we can choose to focus on the *process*, to enjoy each moment, not just the end result. Whether we're driving home a business deal or driving home our daughter from dance class, we're free to choose where to focus our mind.

Where Do *You* Place Your Thoughts?

Scenario #1: Dinner Time

It's dinner time and the *product* is that luscious moment when you sit down with friends and family for a quiet, relaxing dinner, ready to enjoy good food and conversation. The *process*, of course, began hours earlier, when you chose the menu, bought the vegetables, marinated the chicken, boiled the water, cooked the angel hair pasta, prepared the sauce, seasoned the salad.

"If you focus on results, you will never change. If you focus on change, you will get results."
-- Jack Dixon

Scenario #2: Hanging a Bedroom Shelf

It's Saturday afternoon and your daughter bids an hour of your time to hang a bedroom shelf, to house trinkets and such. The *product* is that rarified moment when the shelf is up, perfectly level and fit to store the nick-nacks. The *process*, though a simple one, houses numerous steps -- finding the tools (for me, never an easy task), measuring, drilling, inserting (the toggle bolts), leveling and adjusting (I know, I skipped a few steps. But hey, this is not my forte).

Scenario #3: Planting Tulips

It's late October -- prime time for planting tulips in the yard. The *product* is crystalline, tulips nestled in the ground with a light dusting of mulch to protect them over the winter. The *process*, of course, is multi-layered -- choosing which bulbs to plant, determining the size of the area, laying out the shape of the bed, digging it, improving the soil, planting the bulbs and covering them.

At times like these -- preparing dinner, hanging a

shelf and planting tulips -- our mind tends to spend a disproportionate amount of time *thinking about the product,* that is, about *finishing.* The notion is that if we move swiftly through these chores, we can move on to *more enjoyable tasks.*

Rule 5 encourages us to enjoy seasoning the salad as much as eating it, to enjoy leveling the shelves as much as hanging them, to enjoy selecting the bulbs as much as planting them.

"If you surrender completely to the moments as they pass, you live more richly those moments."
-- Anne M. Lindbergh

In short, Rule 5 urges us to slow down and enjoy that which stands before us. Think about it, how many moments of your *thought life* have you been preoccupied with the outcome? To fairly answer that question, try asking yourself this one:

> *"When I'm engaged in an activity, how much of the time am I thinking about the product (i.e., finishing the task), and how much of the time am I simply enjoying the process?"*

I Can't Wait

"Enjoy the journey, enjoy every moment, and quit worrying about winning and losing."
-- Matt Biondi

Let's face it, we spend a fair piece of time doing things that we don't altogether enjoy. We're forever telling ourselves: "I can't wait until . . . it's Friday . . . it's vacation time . . . the presentation is finished . . . the bills are paid . . . the laundry is folded . . . the house is clean . . . the class is over . . . the beds are made . . . the weeds are gone." But the more obsessed we become with the *product* the less chance we have to enjoy the *process.*

That's not to say we should forsake *pursuing* products. I'm strongly in favor of setting goals (see Rules 18-20) and working hard to achieve them. I love a well-crafted plan to scale mountains. Let's face it, it feels good to clean off your desk, to organize the kitchen, to

Challenge 5A
In Search of the Happy Moment

Think back to your last trip home from the office. What were you thinking about?

Chances are that you spent a portion of your time thinking about the *product*, that is, about that "Happy Moment" -- the moment you walk through the door, hang up your coat and open the fridge for a glass of ice tea (or, perhaps, something stronger). Ahhhhhh, at long last, the "Happy Moment" had arrived.

Don't be fooled! "Happy Moments" are illusory because, more often than not, they turn out to be just that -- brief moments in time that, too quickly, are overwhelmed by a swirl of fresh demands. Once in the kitchen, a stack of mail reminds you that the bills are overdue; an empty milk carton signals that the shelves are bare, and, suddenly, the "Happy Moment" dissolves into a series of new demands, into a series of new products and processes.

Here, then, is the dilemma: by waiting for the "Happy Moment," we wind up *waiting to be happy,* we end up telling ourselves: *when that moment arrives, THEN I'll be happy and not a moment sooner.*

So, please, *don't wait to be happy.* Be happy now, and know that happiness surrounds us . . . if only we open our eyes.

send off the proposal, to arrive at the hotel, to put dinner on the table, to mail in your taxes, to (finally!) place the pictures in the photo album.

But there's a huge difference between *pursuing a product* and *focusing our mind's thoughts on that product.*

"Often the search proves more profitable than the goal."
-- E.L. Konigsburg

Daily, we are lulled into believing that:

Products = Happiness and that . . .

Process = Drudgery

Nonsense.

Do you know anyone who enjoys cooking? I love to watch both my sister-in-law Carole and my brother-in-law Bruce take equal pleasure in the *product* (bringing dinner to the table) and the *process* -- selecting the recipe, gathering the ingredients, creating the sauce, seasoning the pasta, and the meats, and the vegetables. Like many talented chefs, Carole and Bruce have learned to enjoy the *process* as much as (if not more than) the *product*.

This then is our challenge -- to enjoy the *means* as much as the *end*, to accept the notion that the process is not just a road sign, it's the road.

We all know that products bring us pleasure and reward us in infinite ways, but *because our thoughts determine what kind of life we lead,* we must find ways to more thoroughly enjoy the process. Imagine if a runner experienced the same joy in taking a stride as in crossing the finish line.

"Passion doesn't look beyond the moment of its existence."
-- Christian N. Bovee

Does this sound impossible?

My daughter Melyssa would say no, arguing that, despite a societal preoccupation with "products" (of both kinds), it's theoretically possible to enjoy every process. Of course, striving to achieve "products" isn't inherently evil; it's only a problem when it blinds us to the process, when it leads us to pick the roses from the garden without even smelling them.

Enjoy the Ride

Religious maxims remind us that life itself is a pro-cess -- "life is a journey, not a destination." And daily, we're reminded to "enjoy the ride." Nonetheless, we often forget that the bus ride to the amusement park (*process*) can be just as enjoyable as the amusement park itself (*product*), if only we let it (children on a field trip are quick to point out that the bus ride is often the most enjoyable part).

One of my lightbulb moments occurred some years ago on my way to Baltimore, to watch the Orioles play baseball. I was traveling with three of my friends when the conversation turned to traffic. That particular day it was bumper-to-bumper and our collective frustration was apparent (*". . . we should have left earlier"* and *"look at that idiot crossing lanes"*). Mentally, I started to record the conversation and realized that more than 30% of it was devoted to traffic. Ouch!

"Lord, how the day passes! It is like a life, so quickly when we don't watch it, and so slowly if we do."
-- John Steinbeck

So I tried a little thought experiment and placed the four of us at a corner booth at the local restaurant. I imagined we were noshing on chips and sipping margheritas, laughing and telling jokes, simply enjoying one another's company. Chances are slim, as we sat there eating potato skins, that the conversation would turn to traffic (after all, we were sitting in a restaurant). Yet, here we were, four friends together, on the way to a ballgame, consumed by talk about lane changes and arrogant drivers.

The problem, of course, wasn't the traffic at all -- the problem was how we *thought* about it. Now I'll be the first to admit that a highway's visual cues are compelling, that it's hard not to get riled up when you see manic drivers trying to make their way where no car should ever go; but these visual cues need not destroy the *process* (enjoying time with good friends), even as we strive to reach the *product* (arriving at the ballpark).

Finding Pleasure in Everything You Do

So the next time you're on a late night run to the supermarket, try not to be so intent on returning home (*product*) that you fail to enjoy the process -- listening to the car radio, sharing a story with the checkout attendant, passing a friendly word to a neighbor.

Challenge 5B
The Cycle Never Ends

The remarkable part of the Product-Process Connundrum is that the cycle never ends, that is, every *product* has a *process*, and, in turn, every *process* can be subdivided into an endless string of mini-products and processes. For example, once we decide to marinate the chicken (our latest *product*), an entirely new *process* magically unfolds: selecting the marinade, deciding what ingredients to add, finding the brush to spread it, turning the chicken over, checking back in an hour or two to reapply, and so on, and so forth.

The point is, the cycle never ends -- we set our sights on a *product* and a *process* unfolds. And, once engaged in the process, a new product appears. The cycle continues until, fatigued from thought, we decide to stop thinking about them.

And the next time that you're heading home from work, try not to be so intent on pulling into the driveway (*product*) that you neglect to enjoy the trip home. Imagine the walk to your car as part of your exercise program; think of a friendly word to the parking attendant as a bid to connect; consider that an endless traffic jam offers more time to enjoy a radio segment that you otherwise might have missed.

And the next time that you move into a new home, try not to be so focused on putting everything away (*product*) that you miss a chance to embrace the process -- the memories that flow from unpacking sentimental treasures; that warm feeling from watching family members work together; the dreams that flow from imagining what a new home will look like, will become.

"Do not think that what your thoughts dwell upon is of no matter. Your thoughts are making you."
-- Bishop Steere

Grant Yourself Permission

Believe it or not, you're actually allowed -- yes, you're actually permitted -- to enjoy your new home *from the moment that you move in.* You don't have to wait until the carpets are cleaned, or the woodshop is ready, or the bags are unpacked. The fact is, there's no required waiting period . . . for pleasure to begin.

So don't wait . . . to be happy. Don't wait . . . until the product is achieved. Feel good, *right now*. Realize that as soon as the process begins, you're free -- truly free, to enjoy every part of the experience.

Enjoy . . . the process.

Challenge 5C: Creating a Trigger

If you wish to spend more time enjoying the process, try the "trigger" challenge. It's nothing dramatic -- it simply encourages us to create some form of visual, auditory or kinesthetic "trigger" to help shift our thoughts to the process.

Creating a trigger, of course, won't magically transform your thoughts or behavior. And no trigger can quickly induce human change -- only awareness can do that. But a trigger, nonetheless, can help us speed along the *process.*

A personal trigger might be nothing more than a word (spoken internally), a movement or a sound. A trigger need only remind us to stop fixating on the product and begin enjoying the process. The best triggers, of course, are the ones that we create, and the more active the better. I suppose that the ideal trigger would activate all of our senses. But I'm proposing something more modest. I'm proposing a trigger that is equal parts simple and swift.

Here's what I do: when I find my thoughts locked on the product, I clench my hand into a fist (*product*) and slowly open it up (*process*). The hand flex, which takes all of five seconds, reminds me to shift my focus from the product (my fist) to the process (my fingers). If I have an extra moment, I try to roll my fingers out slowly, as if each one represents a part of the process. I imagine taking pleasure in every step. And, if I'm lucky, my thoughts begin to shift away from the product . . . if only for a while.

If you're thinking about creating your own personal trigger, I'd recommend that you: 1. keep it simple; 2. engage your senses; and 3. recognize that you may have to change it at some point, to avoid embarrassing moments (clenching your fist at the next board meeting might be a touch uncomfortable).

Challenge 5D
"I can't wait until . . . "

Have you ever said to yourself . . .

> *"I can't wait until this report is finished."*
> *"I can't wait until the boxes are unpacked."*
> *"I can't wait until the kitchen is cleaned up."*
> *"I can't wait until school is out."*
> *"I can't wait until the presentation is completed."*
> *"I can't wait until I've finished painting the basement."*
> *"I can't wait until the party is over."*

There are times when we say these words with enthusiasm *("I can't wait until the show tomorrow night")*, when our excitement about the *product* (watching the show) actually enhances our enjoyment of the *process* (looking forward to it).

But. more often than not, the phrase: *"I can't wait . . . ,"* signals sorrow, not joy. The phrase typically flows from frustration, from a desire to complete the dreaded task so that other pursuits can be enjoyed -- e.g., music, television, eating, socializing, reading, going to the theater, or attending a sporting event.

Wishing Them Away

Sadly, a remarkable amount of our mental life is spent hoping the unpleasant tasks before us (more accurately, those tasks we've decided are unpleasant) will be done. Privately we think about how good it will feel to be *finished*, how pleased we will be when the . . . filing is done . . . the mail is sorted . . . the proposal is complete.

How then, do we learn to enjoy the filing, to take pleasure in sorting the mail, to enjoy preparing the proposal, not simply completing it?

To do so, to more thoroughly enjoy the process, we must first become aware of our thoughts, and the degree to which we equate products with happiness and process with drudgery. *(continued)*

Here, then, is our three-part challenge:

Part 1. Select one (yes, just one) unpleasant task, that is, a task you don't particularly enjoy doing, the kind that quickly stirs up negative thoughts inside of you.

Part 2. The next time you begin this task, consciously decide to "watch your thoughts," that is, to listen to your private thoughts as you begin the activity; then start doing the activity.

Step 3. As you're "thought watching*," ask yourself three questions to reveal your product-process orientation:

Q1: How often do I think about finishing? (frequency)
Q2: How strong are these feelings? (emotion)
Q3: How long do these thoughts last? (persistence)

The good news is . . . you'll have plenty of chances to run these "thought experiments." Or maybe that's the bad news.

---

* *"Thought watching" is a challenging endeavor because our thoughts tend to loop, as if on a "thought wheel." A thought rises, from any number of sources, quickly peaks in intensity, lays dormant for a while, only to rise again, somewhat less intensely than before.*

The Author's Friends Share Their Thoughts
In a bid to learn how others think, the author assembled a panel of 30 friends (psychologists and social workers among them) to answer some of life's most penetrating questions. Excerpts of their answers appear here.

The author asked his friends:
What tasks are hard for you to enjoy?

"I find it extremely difficult to enjoy cooking 'on the run,' that is, running in after work and running to change and get dinner cooking. It is unpleasant because I really love to cook, but don't want to feel rushed and unable to be 'creative' about cooking. . . .

"Also, I cannot enjoy some of the daily tasks that I have to do with my Mother (i.e. getting her ready for bed). This hangs over my head until she is upstairs and in her bed. I can't relax and enjoy my evening because I know that this chore is coming up. Can't explain it!!" -- Carole E.

* * *

"I hate cleaning house. Oh, I like a neat house. And I'm embarrassed if anyone comes to my door when I'm not expecting them. My tolerance for clutter is higher than most males. So, I allow myself to avoid the unpleasant task of cleaning house. There is NO enjoyment in it for me during the process and little after it's done." -- Nat E.

* * *

"Lightly unpleasant: paying bills (the best part is when it's over -- it's not really the money spending aspect, it's the chore/gotta do drudgery aspect); supremely unpleasant: counseling out or terminating employees (fortunately, not very regular), especially if others than myself should have been providing more constructive feedback prior to the situation reaching this necessity." -- Joel R.

* * *

"Phone calls to difficult customers; any kind of tax (Fed/State) preparation; delivering bad news to anyone." -- Mickey F.

* * *

"Unsavory Tasks: The only thing that I would categorize this way is the homework/ studying required for my Statistics (sadistics) class which I am currently taking in my MBA program. It is very demanding and the subject matter is one about which I do not particularly care. However, I remind myself that it will soon be over . . . and that there are others suffering through it as well. A method I frequently employ to get me through this and other unsavory tasks is to remind myself that it could always be much worse.

"For instance, despite the fact that I have no interest in Statistics, I am able to do the homework and pass the exams. It would be extremely unpleasant if I were less intelligent and not able to grasp the concepts of this required course. The most common thing about which I constantly remind myself is that I am not in war. I try to revisit the feeling that I had after seeing 'Saving Private Ryan' or a documentary I recently saw about P.O.W.'s in Vietnam called 'Return With Honor.' Though

51

Q: *What tasks are hard for you to enjoy?* (continued)

this does not allow me to 'enjoy' an unsavory task, it gets me through it with minimal complaint." -- Chris W.

* * *

"Now if I could only find the silver lining in scrubbing the shower stall." -- Vicki S.

* * *

"Cleaning out the kitty litter used by our two cats." -- Allan H.

* * *

"I dislike making my bed. I don't like to do weekend chores, e.g., fixing things, painting, etc. -- avoid as long as possible. I don't like to get up early -- do it for business meetings or to get Max to school." -- Carl E.

* * *

"I have a difficult time enjoying anything that has bad smells associated with it. You probably do not need details here." -- Karin U.

* * *

"The routine tasks that are performed in a hurry (cleaning, laundry, grocery shopping) can be enjoyable when not in a hurry. It's not always the task that is unpleasant but the context in which it is being performed. . . . I think the context is much more important, in general, than the places and activities. Think about doing something routine by yourself, with someone you don't particularly care for, and with a long lost friend! It dramatically changes the 'fun-ness' of the activity because the activity is no longer the main focus. Companionship, compatibility, laughter take over." -- Marley C.

* * *

"Unsavory Tasks: totally unpleasant is confrontation of any kind. Although I have gotten better at handling it I always have sick feeling in my stomach before, during and after a confrontation with someone. Even if it turns out OK. Somewhat related is meeting or facing strangers -- lots of anxiety there, unless they are totally on my turf where I have some experience or expertise. Don't get me wrong, I definitely enjoy people, it just takes me time to feel comfortable and perhaps trusting of them." -- Vicki H.

* * *

"Unsavory Tasks: thinking of what to make for lunches or dinner. I love making the food. I just hate deciding what to make." -- Gail C.

Pure Outcome
"Very few moments are
perceived as pure outcome."
-- Hugh Prather

Rule #6

Pause

"Nothing valuable can be lost
by taking time."
-- Abraham Lincoln

I used to joke that America's urban residents were all communists because everyone I knew was rushin'. The quip still draws moderate laughter but the underlying themes do not. Nearly 30 years after Alvin Toffler penned *Future Shock*, his prophecies are ringing true -- life is indeed speeding up.

And it's not a pretty sight.

In today's up-tempo technologically driven society we rush about mercilessly. Physically, we drive ourselves to fatigue, traipsing cross-town and cross-country. Mentally, we drive ourselves to distraction, creating a neural web of roles and responsibility. Increasingly, our desire to arrive at the next station stop is so powerful that we fail to notice the fruit stands and chestnut oaks that line our path.

"Our patience will achieve more than our force."
-- Edmund Burke

How do we slow the pace?

By recognizing that the external world will neither wait for us nor slow to meet our needs. More than a century after Alexander Graham Bell's invention altered the nature of human communication, a profusion of choices confront us -- voice mail and e-mail, cell phones and pagers, faxes and wireless Internet connectivity. We thrill at the sound of a wireless connection and praise the e-Gods for delivering faster hookups and high-speed data lines. But have they enhanced our quality of life? Have we gained more than we've lost from these high-tech treats?

Paradoxically, many of the world's technological innovations threaten to dissolve the very resource that they sought to create: time. And, from all appearances, no tool has yet to appear on the technological horizon to turn that tide. Which leaves us with little choice. If we wish to downshift, slow the tempo, our best chance is to turn inside. We need better filters, better screens; we need ways to manage the staggering amount of incoming cerebral traffic. In a word, we need to learn how to pause.

"The time to relax is when you don't have time for it."
-- Sidney J. Harris

Calming Down The Amygdala

Brain researchers have confirmed what we long have known intuitively -- that there's a physiological benefit to pausing. Remember how your parents would tell you to "count 'til 10" when you became angry? Do you know why that works? It has to do with how your brain is wired. When a crisis erupts, roughly 10% of your neurons are routed directly to the amygdala, your brain's emotional center. The other 90% are routed through the cerebral cortex, the "thinking" part of your brain. Scientists believe that we're wired this way for survival, that is, part of our brain is designed to simply "react," even before we "think." By counting to 10, it allows those neurons that first traveled to the amygdala to re-route and go through the cerebral cortex. That is, it gives us time to "think."

A Critical Skill

Pausing is another of those critical life skills that school fails to address ("listening" tops that list, see Rule 11). And it's not the easiest skill to learn. Pausing is difficult to improve because we live in an age which praises speed and glorifies productivity.

But learning to pause is worth the investment. It gives us time to reassess our options, to choose our words and actions more wisely. Pausing gives us time to catch our breath, physically and metaphorically, to idle our engine, if only for a moment, before we speed off in a thousand new directions. A pause may last just a second or two (though a week-long pause sounds somewhat appealing), but whatever the length, each time we choose to pause, we give ourselves a priceless gift -- the gift of time.

Try it out. The next time you step into your car, try pausing, for just a second or two, before you turn on the engine, flip on the radio or hook up your seatbelt. Pause, take a deep breath.

And tonight, when you slip into bed, pause for just a moment before you reach for the book on your night stand. Throughout the day, try pausing . . . before you dial the phone or pour yourself a cold one, before you say no to your kids or yes to a volunteer request. Soon enough you'll find that, simply by pausing, you've created space for yourself that you never knew existed.

"Patience is the ability to idle your motor when you feel like stripping your gears."
-- Barbara Johnson

Rushing is Optional

Think back to a recent time when you were rushing about. Chances are, the matter wasn't urgent, that is, there was no medical emergency or life-threatening situation. The fact is, when we review life's moments, we find that only a handful *demand* an up-tempo pace, a quick reaction or an instantaneous reply. Nonetheless, our personal mantra is one of speed and haste, and soon we forget that rushing is an option.

So . . .

> *. . . the next time you're listening to someone you love, try pausing before you speak, long enough to hear your private thoughts;*
>
> *. . . and the next time you sit down to do the bills, try pausing, long enough to hear your worries and your fears.*

Chances are that if you take the time to pause, you'll quickly learn how powerful five seconds can be.

"In any contest between power and patience, bet on patience."

-- W.B. Prescott

Tomorrow's pressures will come soon enough. There will be a moment, or two, when your emotional center is fully charged. When this moment arrives, consider Rule 6. It's a physiological fact that a momentary stoppage in play -- be it a 20-second timeout or a full one -- will give you enough time to engage the thinking part of your brain. The good news is that in life, unlike basketball, you don't run out of timeouts.

Well, not exactly.

**For more, see Appendix B,
"Learning to Pause" (p193)**

Challenge 6A
Create A Personal Trigger

Today will be no different. Today you'll say more than 10,000 words and make more than 1,000 decisions. And though most will be "automatic," a small handful will have a major impact, on your self-esteem, your relationships and your life direction.

Choose wisely. But choose slowly. Pausing is always in season, but never more so that when we speak and when we decide.

Imagine if, inside your neural network, you were able to build an autonomic mechanism for pausing. If you built such a system, your words would more likely inspire than irritate . . . your decisions based more on intelligence, not impulsivity.

So try creating a mental trigger for pausing, that is, a system that instructs you to pause . . . before you speak. And pause . . . before you decide.

Your "trigger" might be . . .

- ◆ **Physical** . . . placing a finger to your lips;
- ◆ **Visual** . . . imaging waves that come shore; or
- ◆ **Auditory** . . . hearing a voice that simply whispers "wait."

The trick is to find a trigger that works for you, one that fits comfortably into your thought pattern and your mental scheme. Experiment, have fun, be playful. Then, if you find one that works, try to make it a permanent part of your *process*. If you do, the benefits will last a lifetime.

The Author's Friends Share Their Thoughts
In a bid to learn how others think, the author assembled a panel of 30 friends (psychologists and social workers among them) to answer some of life's most penetrating questions. Excerpts of their answers appear below.

The author asked his friends:

How often do you pause?

"Pausing. Whew what a concept. If ever there were a person who was in need of this concept, it must be me.

"Realizing that and then moving on it is another matter indeed. Prather's words* are not easily adhered to (for me at least). I truly believe I am at times almost 'ADD' in my thinking patterns. I have read and re-read Prather's words. Am still not fully understanding them, but will attempt to make the two day exercise."

"Will get back to you in three days time (hopefully). Send search teams if you haven't heard from me in three days. -- Mickey F.

* * *

"I have been told that meditation makes us aware of our thinking as being like frames in a movie, with ever growing gaps between each frame/thought until it is more gap than frame. Pause. Always insights seem to come when we 'day dream' -- they seem to require the pause (that refreshes . . .)." -- John N.

Patience
"Only those who have the patience to do simple things perfectly will acquire the skill to do difficult things easily."
-- Johann Friedrich Von Schiller

The Most Important Talent?
"If I have made any valuable discoveries, it has been owing more to patient attention than to any other talent."
-- Sir Isaac Newton

---

*Hugh Prather, in his book "Notes on How to Live in This World and Still Be Happy," offers tips on learning to pause. Excerpts appear in Appendix B.

Rule #7

Laugh

*"People who laugh actually live longer
than those who don't laugh. Few persons
realize that health actually varies
according to the amount of laughter."*
         -- Dr. James Walsh

It's official. The statistics are in. Laughter heals.

Three decades of research have confirmed what Norman Cousins knew instinctively -- that laughter works. It lowers blood pressure, reduces your heart rate, boosts your immune system and helps you cope with pain.

As if that's not enough, laughter also improves relationships, builds trust among allies and enemies, and helps conquer fears and anxieties. And though no physician will prescribe it, and no pharmacy stocks it, it's quite possible that a daily dose of laughter is nature's perfect medicine, a natural healer.

"Against the assault of laughter, nothing can stand."
         -- Mark Twain

More than 30 years ago Norman Cousins combined his extraordinary intuition and courage to stake claim to the notion that laughter is, indeed, the best medicine. Cousins theorized, then proved, that a regular dose of laughter would remove the cancer from his body. Cousins became living testimony to the mind-body connection, demonstrating beyond a shadow of a doubt that humor heals.

Since Cousins' pioneering work, researchers the

world over have affirmed the power of laughter. Countless studies confirm that laughter creates measurable physiological changes in the human body. A sampling of study results shows that jovial bursts can:

- Relieve pain -- laughter helps patients cope with pain -- laughter releases endorphins, the body's natural pain killers;
- Lower your heart rate -- "When we laugh, our heart rate increases; when we finish laughing, it then decreases to a rate slower than before we started to laugh.";
- Relax your muscles -- "Tension in our muscles increases when we laugh and lessens once we're done.";
- Improve breathing -- "Increased respiration from laughing clears out the dead spaces in our lungs, areas that normally don't get oxygenated"; and
- Boost your immune system[1].

"Time spent laughing is time spent with the Gods."

-- Japanese proverb

Life's Natural Resource

And the body of research continues to grow, confirming what we sense intuitively, that the ability to exercise our inner clown directly affects our ability to enjoy life.

---

[1] *Dr. Mel Borins, author of "An Apple A Day: A Holistic Health Primer," reports: "An interesting study was done around immunoglobulin A, a substance found in your saliva and the first defense your body has against viruses and bacteria. A group of people were given a funny video to watch, while another group watched a documentary. Afterwards, both groups were tested and those who had watched the comedy had higher levels of immunoglobulin A." Dr. Borins adds: "A similar study was also conducted on people who had survived a heart attack. They were given a funny video to watch every day for one year. These people had less complications and lived longer than those who had not watched the videos."*

Start to Laugh

So the next time you're gripped with frustration,

or a case of ill-will,

start to laugh;

And the next time your voice begins to soar,

and your nerves begin to fray,

start to laugh.

"Laughter is the most healthful exertion."
-- C. Wilhelm Hufeland

Buy whimsical books, watch frivilous comedies. Visit comedy clubs and read cartoons. Make funny faces in the mirror. Whatever your fancy, make time in your busy schedule to laugh.

It's powerful medicine.

Challenge 7A
Laughing all the way . . . to work

You probably think that I'm making this up, but at one time, licensed psychologist Phyliss Shanken was employed as a "humor consultant" (currently, she's the Director of Psychological Services at INTROSPECT of BuxMont, www.pshanken.com). But don't let that fool you -- she's an expert on laughing. Below, Phyliss shares her own story, and in so doing, challenges each of us to "laugh ourselves silly."

Phyliss, show us the way.

> *"Every morning, on the way to my office, when I reach the traffic light at Five Points Plaza, I start to laugh. It takes about three to four minutes to drive from there to my office, and I continue to laugh heartily the entire time. I'm alone in the car; no one has told me a joke, 91 FM radio is probably reporting depressing news or guests on a talk show are discussing problems in the world today. Yet, I laugh. In order to start myself off, I don't even try to think of anything funny. I just break into guffaws. If people in other cars give me wide-eyed stares, I just laugh more. After all, embarrassment breeds laughter.*

> *"Why do I put myself through this chortling workout? Because I know that, according to Dr. William Fry, a Stanford psychiatrist who has been a student of laughter for three decades, laughing 100 times a day (about three minutes) is the cardiovascular equivalent of 10 minutes of rowing. Just think of it -- all that healthy stuff without the sweat. And: You don't need water. You don't even need a boat!*

> *"By the end of the three minutes, I feel lighter, less stressed and better able to concentrate. And, like magic, creative ideas start popping up in my mind. Laughter does that to you: HAHA turns into AHHA! I invite you to try laughing yourself silly on command. You'll probably feel foolish at first. But, guess what? That's good. Because you'll laugh more. Once you start to laugh, even if there's nothing funny going on, it gets easier to escalate your merriment. Because of your body's reaction, you feel buoyant. Suddenly, everything starts sounding funny."*

The Author's Friends Share Their Thoughts
In a bid to learn how others think, the author assembled a panel of 30 friends (psychologists and social workers among them) to answer some of life's most penetrating questions. Excerpts of their answers appear below.

The author asked his friends:
Does laughter, and smiling, make you feel better?

The author then challenged his friends to conduct two experiments:

Experiment #1: Smile. "The next time that you're alone -- driving in the car, in the elevator, the bathroom, walking to meet someone, wherever -- try smiling for 10 seconds and see how you feel."

Experiment #2: Laugh. "The next time that you're alone -- you pick the place -- try laughing out loud for 10 seconds. Then see how you feel."

"Did the experiments. I felt lighter and happier in each instance. There was a feeling of less heaviness or less seriousness, yet my surroundings had not changed. There seems to indeed be an internal mechanism that works with this connection." -- Bobbi C.

* * *

"I do believe [in the power of laughter]. I think, in addition to being physically therapeutic, there is also the psychological component of how we feel with those with whom we can laugh. It implies a comfort level, a relaxed atmosphere, and a certain level of trust. That, too, is healthy! There's nothing like a good laugh.

". . . One of the drawbacks of being young is the lack of confidence resulting in taking oneself too seriously. (There are advantages to getting older!)

". . . Think about how exciting it is to hear a baby laugh out loud! Tyler, our new grandson, has just begun to laugh and his Uncle Adam, my other son, flipped when he first heard it. He practically did headstands to make it happen again." -- Marley C.

*"Laughter is
the music of life."
-- Sir William Osler*

Rule #8

Create New Habits

"Your net worth to the world is usually determined by what remains after your bad habits are subtracted from your good ones."
-- *Benjamin Franklin*

We were out to dinner one Friday night when a friend of mine nonchalantly shared this personal insight: "I've decided that I have too many bad habits." I don't think the salad had even arrived when he began to explain: "I spend too much time reading peer reports . . . and too much time reviewing my students' papers, correcting every last detail."

Naturally, in the days that followed, I started to think about my own bad habits and, in an informal way, began to mentally catalogue them. How confronting! As the list grew, I began to think about ways to eliminate them -- perhaps a week-long retreat, a multi-step program, or a series of thought tapes to guide me into new patterns of thought. A plethora of journals and seminars stood ready to help me "kick the habit," "quash the negative behavior" or simply "quit." Volumes were at my fingertips, instructing me on how to stop:

"Laws are never as effective as habits."
-- *Adlai E. Stevenson*

- smoking
- being a doormat;
- abusing caffeine;
- overeating;
- being a reckless driver; and
- drinking.

But there was nothing on *creating* new habits.

The literature was predominantly negative -- heavy on ways to change what's wrong, light on ways to shape what's right. Somehow, the word "habit" was exclusively linked to the negative, much like the word diet is now synonymous with weight loss. But habits can be a good thing, as the authors at www.the-ultimate.com explain:

> *"The simple notion that habit is a bad thing is that of total ignorance. . . . The fact is that 95% of what we do from one day to the next is in repetition. Understanding this may put our whole perspective into a different view. We should now be able to see that since habit governs so much, all we have to do is force ourselves to do the things we want . . . and need to do, on a regular basis. This automatically becomes a habit of choice and something that can be constructive instead of destructive."*

"Good habits are formed; bad habits we fall into."
-- Source Unknown

Unfortunately, most of us simply aren't in the habit of creating new ones. Instead, we tend to focus on eradicating bad ones. But imagine if you decided to sit down and consciously *create* a new habit (*"hmmm, what habit would I like to begin?"*), a new way of behaving that we know would bring pleasure to us and those around us. Imagine.

Rule 8 urges us to do just that, to spend more time creating than destroying, more time building than dissolving. To fully invest in Rule 8, we need to dismiss the notion that habits are, in and of themselves, negative creatures. They're not. Habits are positive elements in our lives, the lifeblood of our actions, and interactions, and the more energy we invest in creating new ones, the more excitement, and less drudgery, enters our world.

So let's advance this new philosophy -- that habits must be made, even before they can be broken -- with six foundational guideposts.

Guidepost #1: You're Not Alone

It seems trite to say, but everyone has bad habits -- ongoing, unwise behaviors that significantly interfere with our relationships, our job, our social life and our ability to manage our internal affairs. Some people drink too much, some people talk too much. Others neglect, or abuse, their bodies or neglect their spiritual life. Most of us procrastinate.

But when we look at our habits it's important to remember that we're not alone, that every one of our fellow travelers, all seven billion of us, have habits that are objectionable.

Guidepost #2: Habits Are Made To Be Broken

"Good habits are as easy to form as bad ones."

-- Tim McCarver

Dr. John Feldmeier's message is simple, yet eloquent -- the past does not equal the future. Listen to an exercise that he puts his students through, and realize how appropriate it is for all of us, every day.

". . . I want you to find a pencil or pen so you can write down what I'm about to say. Ready, please write this down. The past does not equal the future. Once again, the past does not equal the future. Next, I want you to take what you have written down and place it where you will see it each and every day. Okay, what does it mean? It means those poor study habits, such as not completing assignments, missing classes, and staying up too late before your next class, do not have to be repeated in the future. Who can make these changes? Yes, you're correct. You, and only you, can change the future to achieve more success and productivity. Remember, don't let the past be your future. Make these changes for a better life."

Guidepost #3: Feed the positive, starve the negative

Dr. Phil Shapiro *(www.philipshapiro.com)* encourages us to "nourish the positive habit and starve the negative habit." He explains: "Keep feeding the positive habit to make it stronger and starving the negative habit to make it weaker. Give the best of your effort, concentration, and attention to the new habit until it takes over and becomes a natural, effortless, and automatic part of your repertoire. Keep battling and you will win. Craving ceases. Peace and strength deepen. Life becomes easier and more natural."

"Habit is a form of exercise."
-- Elbert Hubbard

Guidepost #4: You Don't Need More Self-Discipline

When we try to create a new habit, or get rid of the "undesirable," how important is self-discipline? Not very, insist the authors at www.prodigy.com, who explain:

"Self discipline is not the key to success. There are millions of unsuccessful people out there who are very self disciplined; they're just disciplined to the wrong set of habits and patterns of behavior, whether by choice or by accident. Perhaps it is better in training in the martial arts to not focus so heavily on achieving this state of self discipline, and instead focus more on changing patterns of behavior and habits.

"You already have all the self discipline you need, you're 100% self disciplined. The problem is, you're disciplined to existing habits and patterns of behavior. If you're not happy with the status quo, it's not a matter of achieving some state of self discipline, it's a matter of changing the status quo and altering those habits. . . . It's

just a matter of exchanging bad habits and pat-
terns for good ones. Granted, most people don't
choose their habits, they fall into them over time,
and it takes great effort to change a habit. It's not
the discipline that makes them change, though,
it's simple determination to do better."

The soothsayers at arrowweb.com agree:

"Focus on habits and forget about dis-
cipline. Everyone is already completely
disciplined . . . to their existing set of habits.
We have work habits, relationship habits,
health habits, and so on. Each of us has a
full set of habits which regulate most of our
behavior. . . . Progress in life is not a result
of more discipline, but rather of developing
goal-directed habits. Are your habits working
for you, or against you?"

> *"Quality of life is not an*
> *act, it is a habit."*
> *-- Aristotle*

Leo Babauta, of zenhabits.net, adds his voice to
the choir:

". . . [D]iscipline is a myth. It might sound
good, but it's not a useful concept. When it
comes to taking specific actions to make your-
self do something, the only things you can do
are motivation. Not discipline. I've challenged
people to come up with a discipline action that
isn't motivation for years now, and no one has
done it."

Guidepost #5: Start Small

Anyone who has picked up a new habit -- exercising
three times a week, overcoming shyness, hanging up
their clothes immediately after taking them off -- real-
izes how difficult it is to initiate a new behavior.

So take the time to start small -- don't overreach,

don't overshoot, don't overcommit. Instead, start small -- as small as possible -- and build on your successes. Your new exercise program might begin by walking for two minutes the first day. And while two minutes might appear inconsequential, trust me, it's not. Far more important than the time invested is the pattern created, a pattern that may, just may, become a habit that sticks.

Guidepost #6: Don't Turn a Lapse Into a Relapse

How often have you started a new habit, only to see your energy dissipate in just a day or two? At times like these it's critically important to distinguish between a *lapse* and a *relapse.* Trust me, they are not the same. In the book "Managing Your Mind," authors Gillian Butler & Tony Hope offers these words of wisdom:

"The greatest people will be those who possess the best capacities, cultivated with the best habits."
-- James Harris

"The problem with habits is that they are automatic, which means that until they are fully broken they can easily come back. It can be disheartening to have made progress in breaking a habit and then to find that it is back, possibly in full force. It is easy to think that you are back to square one even though you are not. If you have made progress once, you can make progress again, and the second time it will be easier because you have trodden the path before (you've dug the hole). It is helpful to think about why the lapse occurred so that you can learn from this, but the most important thing is to repeat the steps that helped to reduce the habit before. The key to success is to see the present setback as a lapse, not a relapse. The lapse is like falling off your bike: if you pick yourself up and dust yourself off you can continue cycling along."

*Picked Up Any Good Habits Lately?**

If you're in the market for some new habits, why not start here?

- Smiling at people you meet
- Arriving at places on time
- Listening, with intent
- Saying please and thank you

- Visiting the doctor and dentist, for regular checkups
- Learning how to relax
- Keeping a pair of tennis shoes at the office
- Building your confidence (make it a habit)

- Being kind -- to servers and telemarketers
- Putting things away, as soon as you walk in the door
- Exercising -- the right amount
- Locking the car door
- Creating new habits

* Looking for a great list of positive habits? Try Dirk Mathison's book, titled: "The Book of Good Habits -- 2000 simple and creative habits for the mind, health, safety, sex, love, friendship and parenting."

5-Step Challenge for Creating a New Habit ☞

Challenge 8A
Create a New Habit: 5 Simple Steps

You've been thinking about it, I know you have. You'd like to make some changes in your life but aren't sure where to start, or how to go about it. Worry not. Here are five simple steps that will take you there.

Step 1: Know What it Takes

It takes far more than skill to create a new habit -- it takes knowledge and desire as well. Author Steven Covey frames the issue beautifully, explaining that habits "consist of knowledge, skill and desire. Knowledge allows us to know what to do, skill gives us the ability to know how to do it, and desire is the motivation to do it."

Step 2: Select a Specific Habit

When creating a new habit, try to be specific. The habit may relate to your family, your work, your health or your possessions -- no matter. Just make certain that the habit has meaning for you and is something that you would classify as desirable.

Step 3: Think Small

Success breeds success, so think small, think zero to one. Perhaps you'll begin by practicing the piano for 30 minutes per week, or devote 10 minutes every Saturday morning for a journal entry. Too little, you say?

In the business of personal change, it's perfectly clear that the size of the challenge is far less important than *initiating* the challenge, that is, in taking that first step. Equally clear is that devoting a fixed time to nearly ANY task -- on a daily or weekly basis -- will produce enormous changes in the course of a year.

Don't believe me? Then try this mini-challenge: once a week, for the next month, call one person (yes, just one) that you haven't talked to in over a month. Go ahead, try it. For the next four Saturday mornings, after you pour your cup of coffee, flip through your phone book and pick out a person to call (yes, just one). I guarantee that a month from now you'll be impressed by all that's transpired.

Step 4: Write It Down

Believe it or not, one of the most critical steps in achieving our goals is to write them down *(please see the introductory section on goal-setting -- page 149 -- titled "The Perfect Recipe")*. The simple act of putting pen to paper somehow deepens our resolve and our commitment.

Step 5: Respect Physiology

Patience is always an asset, but rarely more so than when trying to change our behavior. Explains neuropsychologist Dr. Michael Gilewski, with the Loma Linda University Health System:

> *"Although multiple aspects of the brain are involved in any activity, the [cerebellum] becomes our 'little friend' when we try to establish a habit. . . . One-third of the brain's billions of neurons -- cells that conduct the brain's primary functions -- are tightly packed into this small section located at the base of the brain."*

> *By analyzing the function of the cerebellum, Gilewski learned that there's no neurological or psychological shortcuts available. He explains: "New habits are fragile and are nurtured by continued success in achievement. . . . Despite the ploy of a TV or magazine ad toward a speedy health goal, there is no quick way to establish habits, given their neurological and psychological complexity. . . . By establishing one healthy habit at a time, each will become a foundation for the next."*

More on habits:
- *"Too Many Bad Habits?" (see Appendix C, page 195); and*
- *"Recruit Strong Partners" (see Appendix D, page 198).*

The Author's Friends Share Their Thoughts
In a bid to learn how others think, the author assembled a panel of 30 friends (psychologists and social workers among them) to answer some of life's most penetrating questions. Excerpts of their answers appear below.

The author asked his friends:
Do you often think about your habits?

"Not enough. I don't spend nearly enough time thinking about either -- creating positive habits or eliminating negative habits. Perhaps the time I spend most thinking of either is Sunday morning. Somehow that's triggered by attending church. Weird. I would like to think I spend more time working on ridding myself of my negative habits --but then I would have to look inwardly and recognize those that I have and that's a scary thought.

"But seriously, we would really like to accomplish such -- ridding ourselves of negative or bad habits and more importantly build upon good ones.

"[I'd say that I spend] 60% of my time dealing with negative habits and 40% on creating new good habits." -- Mickey F.

* * *

"Just a quick thought -- and that is that it seems to me the word routine is now used as the positive side of habit." -- Karin U.

* * *

"Good habit . . . bad habit . . . who put the value on them? If we do them, they're ours, aren't they? And, because they are ours, haven't we in some fashion decided to keep them? I must admit, I don't spend much time at all thinking about habits. . . .

"Who/How can I determine if this behavior is a 'new habit'? At what time did it become something other than something I'm trying and become a habit? Is it a habit when I can't resist it any more? I'm forever picking up new things to do. If I repeat them, are they habits?" -- Nat E.

Smoking
"This [smoking] habit is [old and dear and precious to me] . . . I will grant, here, that I have stopped smoking now and then, for a few months at a time, but it was not on principle, it was only to show off; it was to pulverize those critics who said I was a slave to my habits and couldn't break my bonds." -- Mark Twain

Rule #9

Respect PPIs
(personal preference items)

*"My idea of an agreeable person is a person
who agrees with me."*
                    -- Benjamin Disraeli

It's Friday evening and the dinner party conversation turns to literature. Just two days ago you finished reading "The Beckoning," a novel of widespread acclaim but personal disappointment. You begin sharing your reservations when a forceful personality interrupts and declares, "How could you not like that book? It was . . ."

"I have never in my life learned anything from any man who agreed with me."
-- Dudley Field Malone

It's Wednesday night, at dinner time, when your daughter turns down an offer to try the broccoli bits -- for the 67th time. You inform her that the broccoli bits "truly are delicious" and explain (again) that "if you give them a chance," you'll "find out what you've been missing."

It's Saturday afternoon and you've taken in a rare movie matinee. You're leaving the theatre, reliving the magnificent performance, when you overhear your friend mutter: "What a waste of time." You're stunned, and quickly contemplate whether to: 1. challenge your friend with a sharp-tongued: "What are you talking about? That was a great movie;" or 2. smile, recall Rule 9, and ask your friend what they didn't like about it.

Rule 9 is about respect -- respecting other people's preferences (e.g., in food, clothing, home decorations), other people's likes and dislikes (music, books, movies, hobbies) and other people's choices (friends, mates, lifestyles). Taken together, I call these PPIs, or personal preference items, though in truth PPIs represent more than just "items," they stand for people and feelings as well.

The central notion underlying Rule 9 is that every human brain is unique. Every human brain benefits from unique construction and unique environmental exposure, each of us boasting more than a billion neural connections. That's seven billion brains roaming the planet, each with a billion unique neural connections. You do the math.

"There never was in the world two opinions alike, no more than two hairs or two grains. The most universal quality is diversity."
-- Michel Eyquem De Montaigne

Naturally Different (or, Naturally, Different)

How unique are we? Imagine that you and your closest friends -- in a moment of folly -- agree to have your private thoughts recorded for the next two hours, providing us with a word-by-word, thought-by-thought account of your private musings. If you compared each of the transcripts, it would quickly illustrate the obvious, that each of us is radically different in how we think, what we feel, and how we record life's moments.

But though we accept human "differentness" as natural, we often lapse into believing that other people should like what we like . . .

"I can't believe you don't like that song,"

think like we think . . .

"Why do you want to go there?"

and feel like we feel . . .

"That shouldn't bother you."

How unrealistic.

Let's face it. We're different. We have different opinions, different likes and different feelings than our spouse, our children, our parents, our friends and our peers. Why not accept, enjoy and respect each other's PPIs?

Naturally, there are times when we try to pull others into our "circle of preference," and, in large measure, these moments are harmless. For example, when we turn on our favorite radio station in the car we often encourage fellow passengers to "give it a try," in hopes that they'll come to like it. When they do, we rejoice, knowing that we share another bond together. But when we don't agree -- on TV shows, restaurants and politics (don't get me started) -- we often overreact and fail to celebrate our differences.

"I don't understand you. You don't understand me. What else do we have in common?"
-- Ashleigh Brilliant

Now I'll admit that if you live with other people, the temperature in the living room and the color of the wallpaper are bonafide issues for public debate. But if you stop to actually think about other people's personal preferences you soon realize how few affect us directly. You might not like the color of their shoes, their taste in undergarments, their choice in music or their culinary style. But what does it really matter?

The solution is simple: R-E-S-P-E-C-T. Recently, I ordered three appetizers for dinner instead of the traditional appetizer and entrée. Naturally, my choice had no direct impact on those with whom I was dining, but it certainly left them uncomfortable with my choice.

Our Fragile Ego

Why do people spend so much time convincing others to agree with them, to concur with their choices

Challenge 9A
R-E-S-P-E-C-T = T-C-E-P-S-E-R

Respect, of course, runs both ways.

So when someone . . .

    . . . attacks your favorite TV show;
    . . . knocks your taste in music;
    . . . insists you "at least try" the vegetable dish;
    . . . chides you for watching "Grease" for the 32nd time;
    . . . criticizes *your* choice in hobbies;
    . . . says something snide about the clothes you're wearing,

Tell them to remember Rule #9.

And when *you're* the person who . . .

    . . . attacks someone's choice in entertainment;
    . . . denounces a person's choice in friends;
    . . . mocks a friend about their taste in music;
    . . . criticizes a person's choice in hobbies;
    . . . insists your friend try the chicken soup,

Tell yourself to stop. Then apologize.

"My opinion, my conviction, gains immensely in strength and sureness the minute a second mind has adopted it."
     -- Novalis

and opinions? Psychologists point to our fragile ego and explain that when others agree with us, they validate our opinions and lead us to feel more confident, more self-assured.

Fair enough. We pull others into our "circle of preference" because it *feels* good. But when you're the person being criticized, when your opinions are being rebuked, when your PPIs are being denounced, it doesn't feel particularly good. In fact, it feels kind of irritating, not to mention intrusive and unnecessary.

Granted, it's a delicate balance between legitimately *expressing* one's opinion and *criticizing* another's. Example: say you're shopping with your spouse for a floor covering and you spot an appealing design. You share your opinion, you enthuse and exalt, but your spouse, with their own unique inclinations and dispositions, rebuffs the selection and declares the design not to their liking. What to make of this ever-familiar situation?

Remember that respect does not mean agreement. Respect means respect. Respect means acknowledging that another person feels differently from you; respect means accepting that another person finds certain items appealing even though you might not. Sadly, when two parties disagree, they often fail to maintain their respect for each other's opinion -- they lapse into attacking the other's position, their choice or preference, inferring that their opinion is of little worth, of little value.

"You can always tell when a man's well informed. His views are pretty much like your own."

-- Louis Morris

For a couple, selecting a carpet of mutual desire can be a delicate process of negotiation, as two minds strive to find an item -- a PPI -- upon which they can comfortably agree. *The challenge is to maintain respect for each other's opinion in the midst of an ongoing negotiation.*

Typically, Rule 9 faces its greatest tests in marriage, and it's easy to see why -- sharing is a central tenet of the spousal relationship and the sharing challenges are omnipresent. But Rule 9 is tested in every relationship -- picture two friends, heading down the highway on a week-long vacation. Soon they'll have to share their music. then agree on a lunch stop, a hotel and a sightseeing schedule. Relationships are the perfect test-bed for practicing Rule 9, offering countless opportunities to respect, and meld, PPIs.

How Can You Eat That For Breakfast?

Granted, most violations of Rule 9 are light fare,

as when someone asks: "How can you eat pizza for breakfast?" What they're really saying, of course, is: "I can't conceive of eating pizza for breakfast. How can you?" Certainly, this type of "PPI Challenge" is neither life- nor ego-threatening; nonetheless, people who violate Rule 9 in the kitchen tend to violate it in the bedroom, and the office, and the community center, not to mention the peace table in Geneva.

" I must respect the opinions of others even if I disagree with them."
-- Herbert H. Lehman

The bottom line: Respect PPIs, no matter how heavenly, no matter how mundane. When you respect another person's PPIs -- and acknowledge that their opinion is of equal weight -- you have taken a major step toward human acceptance.

So the next time you hear someone begin their sentence with:

"I can't believe that you . . . "

"How could you . . . "

"You can't possibly . . . "

. . . just smile and tell them that it's a matter of (personal) taste.

Tip Sheet: Think Body Parts

If you're struggling to remember Rule 9, try these three simple tips:

Tip #1: All Palettes Are Not Alike (taste no evil)

Children know this already. Parents offer them food, extol the food's virtues (its taste, its nutritional benefits), but often fail to recall that their child's palette is not the same as theirs. Foods that parents love simply may not work for younger, still-maturing palettes. Throughout life, we're forever confronting the incongruous notion of palette uniformity. Example: your friend orders clam chowder for lunch and, after delighting in the taste, offers you some. You try a spoonful, grimace, and gracefully slide the spoon across the table. If your friend rejoins with: "You mean you don't like it? It's delicious," then they're suffering from a case from APU (Assumed Palette Uniformity). Be kind.

Tip #2: All Eyes Are Not Alike (see no evil)

Hold up a first grader's drawing and ask the young one what she "sees." Inevitably, she sees things we can't imagine, pictures we can't envision. Tip #2 can be read both literally ("seeing" a movie or "reading" a book) and figuratively ("seeing" the special qualities inside a person), because each person's eyes see the world differently, through different lenses, different screens. Each person's unique way of seeing affirms the simple notion that our opinions, our decisions, and our filters are unique. Instead of attacking another person's PPI, try to envision how the other person sees the topic or sees the person. You may just be surprised.

Tip #3: All Ears Are Not Alike (hear no evil)

We listen to the same music but we "hear" different tunes. We listen to our children, to our parents, to our friends, to our neighbors, but we "hear" different themes. For the most part, our ears look the same, but our auditory tracks are not. Learning style research supports what we know intuitively -- that each person's brain chemistry is vastly different from our neighbor's, that some of us receive information more easily through our auditory track than through our visual or kinesthetic track. Lo, inside, we are built differently, though we appear to look the same.

The Author's Friends Share Their Thoughts
In a bid to learn how others think, the author assembled a panel of 30 friends (psychologists and social workers among them) to answer some of life's most penetrating questions. Excerpts of their answers appear below.

The author asked his friends:
Do you respect PPIs?

Author's note: I posed three "situations" to my friends, then asked them: "Can you relate?" Below are the situations, and their comments.

Situation #1

It's Friday evening and the dinner party conversation turns to literature. Just two days ago you finished reading "The Beckoning," a novel of widespread acclaim but personal disappointment. You begin sharing your reservations when a forceful personality cuts in and declares, "How could you not like that book? It was . . . "

Situation #2

It's Wednesday night, dinner time, when your daughter turns down an offer to try broccoli bits -- for the 67th time. You inform her that broccoli bits "truly are delicious" and explain (again) that "if you give them a chance, you'll find out what you've been missing."

Situation #3

It's Saturday afternoon and you've taken in a rare movie matinee. You're leaving the theater, reliving the magnificent performance, when you overhear your friend mutter: "What a waste of time." Stunned, you're left to decide whether to: 1) challenge your friend with a sharp-tongued response; or 2. smile and ask your friend what they didn't like about it.

"Yes, Yes, and Yes. I think most of us suffer from APU (assumed palette uniformity), some obviously more than others. Situation #2 was constant at the dinner table when I was growing up. My mother: "I don't understand. You like tomatoes. Why won't you drink tomato juice?" "It's delicious, just try it." That was enough convincing not to try anything even if it looked good. A power struggle often ensues if we try to force our personal preferences on others, although it depends on the situation.

"If a friend suggests trying something (to eat, perhaps), we might take the plunge sooner than if it's our parent, babysitter, older sibling, etc. It's not about whether we like, want, or are interested in the PP, it's who expresses the preference that drives our decision much of the time.

Do you respect PPIs? (continued)

"If someone recommends a movie to you, doesn't it depend on who does the recommending as to how you receive it? And how they do it? (Usually who they are determines how they do it!)

"Far better to gather one's wits and say, 'Tell me about it. . . . ' when someone expresses a like/dislike. That sends the message that we value their opinion rather than trying to bring them around to our way of thinking. . . . We learn nothing if we take over the conversation, other than the fact that we can articulate our own preferences!

"I do think that there are times when it is appropriate and even important to express our opinion, however, for example, if your child comes home from a party and tells you that everyone was drinking. You might say, 'How did you feel about that?' or you might say, 'That's disgraceful. I know you would never do that.' Sometimes there is a time and place for the latter. Context and timing are everything." -- Marley C.

* * *

"Yes, I can relate, but I think there are subtle differences between exchanges like this among equals, and exchanges like this between parents and children. I think that part of a parent's 'job' is to help kids stretch, and sometimes that means introducing them to broccoli bits." -- Ilene F.

* * *

"What? You mean other people don't always have the same taste as 'I do'?

"Situation #1: I find myself especially taking to heart this one. It made me think "That's just what I have done on more occasions than I care to think about. Gee, I must be a huge bore to friends at times. Why do I do that? I need to stop and think more often . . . before I speak."

"Situation #2: Don't we all do this on occasion to our children. Isn't it almost 'second nature' to do so, thinking it will only benefit them, imposing our 'educated will' upon them? I have memories of sitting at a dinner table with my sister (I think I was about 8 or so) and having our mother decree that we could not move until we ate our peas (both my sister and I had a distinct dislike at that age for peas). Not that it was a traumatic memory, but why do I remember it so to this day?" -- Mickey F.

* * *

"I can relate. But it was not always thus! Not-so-many-years-ago, I would react badly, thinking that my very being was challenged if someone disagreed with me. It was as if there was one set (and only one set) of reactions. If mine disagreed with another's . . . boy! I must be stupid, 'cause I picked the 'wrong' one!

"My advancing years have given me a different perspective. If so inclined, I'll carry on a detached discussion, trying to hear why the other [person] liked/disliked the book and express my views. Sometimes I'll remain so detached, I won't join the fray. But I do allow the different 'palate,' . . . even for me!

"With the broccoli, I DO enter that one. Not to force the palate to change but to get the kid to try. They may NOT like broccoli. I didn't, until I reached 30. My bottom line is that I will respect the kid's opinion if it is based on fact or experience. I will be less receptive if it is based on prejudice. (Is my feeling about this different for kids than adults? Probably so. I'll try harder to 'adjust the palate' of a child than of an adult.)" -- Nat E.

How Arguments and War Begin
"While it seems so fundamental to respect other people's PPIs, I find it a constant struggle to understand why anyone could disagree with my own views, and biases. Intellectually I praise our differences (I can't imagine a world where everyone was the same), but on a personal level I often challenge any opinion that differs from my own. I guess that's how arguments and wars begin."

-- Ron Taylor

Rule #10
Avoid USSs
(unsolicited suggestions)

*"The best advisers, helpers and friends, always are
not those who tell us how to act in special cases,
but who give us, out of themselves, the ardent spirit
and desire to act right, and leave us then, even
through many blunders, to find out what our own
form of right action is."*

　　　　　　　　　　　　　　　-- Phillips Brooks

　"Why don't you tell him it's over?"

　*"Maybe you should call the doctor and check
　it out."*

　"Just tell them you're fed up -- just quit!"

Welcome to the field of Suggestology, the science of
advice, persuasion and exhortation. As practicing sug-
gestologists, each of us, over the course of a day, offers
countless suggestions to friends and family:

*"No one wants advice,
only corroboration."*
　　　-- John Steinbeck

　-- we tell them what to say (*"Just tell him that
　you're not happy"*);

　-- we tell them what to do (*"Go ahead, call her"*);

　-- we tell them how to think and how to feel
　(*"Don't let that bother you"*).

We dispense advice in the lunch room, at the grocery

store and the kitchen table. We rarely shy from telling others exactly what we think they should do, or think, or feel.

But are our suggestions welcome? Are they appreciated?

Suggestions often are unwelcome intrusions in a conversation. When a person shares their frustrations on the job they don't necessarily want someone to tell them that it's time to start looking for a new one. When a person is having trouble in a relationship, they don't necessarily need someone to tell them that it's time to find a new mate. And when a person is disappointed from a poor showing -- in the boardroom or the ballfield -- they don't necessarily need someone to tell them what to do the next time around.

"Advice is seldom welcome; and those who want it the most always like it the least."
-- Lord Chesterfield

There are times, of course, when our suggestions are welcome, when a person seeks our advice, our help, our counsel. But, too often, *we fail to wait for the question,* we neglect to wait for the person to ask: *"What do you think I should do?"* Instead, we barge ahead and dispense our wisdom, neglecting to let the person finish venting, or create a solution on their own. We are, in a word, impatient.

The SS Exchange (Statement . . . Suggestion)

Our impatience manifests itself in what I call the "The SS Exchange" -- that is, a conversational sequence in which a Statement is followed by a Suggestion.

For example, we respond to a statement . . .

> **Statement**: *"I can't stand my boss, he's such a jerk."*
> **Suggestion**: *"Why don't you quit and move on?"*

Remember . . .

♦ When people complain, they don't necessarily want a solution. Sometimes they just want to complain.

♦ When people are troubled, they don't necessarily want a solution. Sometimes they just want to be heard.

♦ When people worry, they don't necessarily want you to solve it. Sometimes they just want to worry out loud.

. . . instead of waiting for the question. If we waited long enough, a question may emerge:

> **Question**: *"My boss is a jerk, do you think I should leave?"*
> **Suggestion**: *"Yes, I think you'll be happier someplace else."*

Each of us is familiar with the the "SS Exchange," alternately dispensing, and receiving, unsolicited suggestions (USSs). The truth is that the "SS Exchange" is so deeply imbedded in our conversational style that we often don't recognize how often we deliver, and receive, suggestions.

> *"To offer a man unsolicited advice is to presume that he doesn't know what to do or that he can't do it on his own."*
> *-- John Gray*

At times the SS Exchange is quite harmless, the suggestion benign:

> **Statement**: *"It was so annoying, I had to wait over an hour at the doctor's office today."*
> **Suggestion**: *"Why don't you switch doctors? I never have to wait."*

But what if you like your doctor? What if you just don't like waiting?

Or imagine that you're out to dinner with friends when you declare:

> **Statement**: *"I can't stand the traffic. It was*

> *backed up for 5 miles this morning."*
> ***Suggestion****: "Why don't you take the bus?*
> *It's air conditioned and it's comfortable."*

But what if you enjoy driving your car? What if you just don't like the traffic?

Suggestions flow freely from our lips, and from the lips of others, and, to be fair, they're usually well-intentioned (*"I just wanted to help."*) But imagine, just imagine, if we waited for our friends to *ask the question* before we offered our advice. A close friend of mine once remarked, *"Wow, what a radical concept . . . actually waiting for someone to ask for advice before offering it!"*

"Most people who ask for advice from others have already resolved to act as it pleases them."
-- Knegge

From time to time, friends and family members *will* ask you a question (I promise), will seek your advice. For example:

> ***Question****: "Do you think I should apply for the job?"* or

> ***Question****: "Where do you think we should go for vacation?"*

At times like these, go for it. But when your friend starts complaining about their job, their love life, their aches and pains, their tennis game, their neighbors -- try *waiting for the question* before offering a ready solution. Too often we fail to pause, and in our rush to help, to instantly make things better, we suggest.

Can You Wait? (it's tough, I know)

Rule 10 urges us to *wait for the question,* to simply *listen* to a friend air their frustrations. Indulge them. Don't try to fix things. *Just listen.*

> ***Statement****: "It was so annoying, I had to*

> *wait over an hour at the doctor's office today."*
>
> **Response***: "That must have been really frustrating, especially when they press you to arrive on time." or*
>
> **Statement***: "I can't stand the traffic when I'm driving to work."*
> **Response***: "That's the worst, isn't it? Sitting in traffic like that."*

By responding, without suggesting, we honor our friends and our family, we make them feel more whole, more valued. This isn't to say that all suggestions are malevolent, they're not; they usually flow from kindness, out of a genuine desire to help friends and family, to ease their angst. But too often we give answers before there are questions, and in so doing, we erode, not evolve, our relationships.

"He who can take advice is sometimes superior to him who can give it."
-- Karl Von Knebel

I'm certain that you could name one or two people who are compulsive USSers, that is, people who are virtually incapable of listening without offering their opinion. Men are particularly skilled at this (but by no means are the sole purveyors), offering advice in place of being an attentive listener.

Parents: Living in the Land of USS

Parents, at every age, are adept at offering USSs (one morning, on the way to school, I asked 14-year-old Olivia to recall any recent USS from my lips; it took her less than two seconds to recount my latest). As parents, we live in the Land of USS for good reason -- we care about our children; we suffer when they hurt (either emotionally or physically) and we worry about their future. This combination of care and worry makes it difficult, at times nearly impossible, to watch errant habits without injecting advice. But as a rule, USSs are unwanted intrusions into their lives and are probably worth avoiding.

Some USSs are direct:
"Why don't you call the teacher and ask her about some extra credit projects?"

While others are more subtle:
"Are you interested in reading this article?"

But subtle or direct, a USS is still a USS. In its place, try uttering these five unambiguous words: *"Would you like a suggestion?"*

From time to time, my wife Roe and I will pose the question to one of our daughters. Invariably, they'll say, "Sure, what is it?" But on occasion, we'll hear a curt, "No, thank you." When I hear these words I usually smile inside because I know that, within a second or two they'll recant and say, somewhat derisively: "OK, go ahead, what is it?" Then we laugh and debate which role is more difficult: having a suggestion and not being able to share it (it's hard, believe me), or choosing not to hear a suggestion that someone has for you. Case in point: just last night, while in the kitchen cleaning up, Natalie was sharing the trials and travails of the day when I offered: "Would you like a suggestion?" Without blinking an eye she said, "No, thank you," and now, 24 hours later, I can't remember what I wanted to suggest.

In Practice

In theory, the concept is irrefutable -- a person should wait for a question before offering an answer. But in practice, it's extraordinarily difficult. Day to day, moment to moment, we're so busy sharing our view of the world, we're so anxious to speak, that we stop listening and, too often, jeopardize our most priceless relationships. So tonight, take Rule 10 to the dinner table with you. Just a suggestion.

Challenge 10A
How Long Can You Wait?

Supplies needed:
- ♦ One stopwatch
- ♦ Two ears
- ♦ Plenty of patience (be sure to bring that with you)

Later today, or perhaps sometime this week, I'd like you to try this three-step experiment. I promise it won't take but a minute or two.

Step #1. Select a conversation to "watch." The conversation can be between you and your spouse, you and a friend, you and a work associate or you and your child. But you're definitely one of the two primary characters. That's a must.

Step #2. As soon as the conversation begins, press your stopwatch. Your challenge? See how long the conversation goes before the person actually *asks you a question about what they should do.*

Step #3. Stop the stopwatch the moment the person asks for your advice. For example, if the person says:

> *"What do you think I should do?"* or
> *"What would you recommend?"* or
> *"Do you think I should go ahead?"*

. . . stop the stopwatch. The challenge is over. You're now free to dispense the advice that you've been holding inside. But please don't cheat. Because if the other person asks:

> *"What have you been up to?"* or
> *"How's the job going?"* or
> *"Are you still playing tennis?"*

. . . that doesn't count. Sure, they asked you a question, but it wasn't about them, it was about you. So no points. Oh, and remember to bring some extra batteries for your stopwatch. You just might need them.

The Author's Friends Share Their Thoughts
In a bid to learn how others think, the author assembled a panel of 30 friends (psychologists and social workers among them) to answer some of life's most penetrating questions. Excerpts of their answers appear below.

The author asked his friends:
Do you receive more USSs than you deliver?
And what's your ratio, that is, delivering vs. receiving?

"60% Deliverer (wow!) That caused a 'back-up' in my psyche . . . and I hate USSs normally. That would mean I receive 40% of the time, correct? Either way, it's too many, too often. I must try and curb my(self)." -- Mickey F.

* * *

"Deliverer vs. Recipient: 80-20" -- Gail C.

* * *

"I deliver as much as I get. In other words, it's as annoying receiving them from other people as I'm sure I am giving them. But I just can't help it. I really believe that people can gain from other people's insights into things or their just simply 'knowing better' or knowing more about a subject." -- Carole E.

* * *

"40-60 at this time. When my children were younger, it was probably the opposite." -- Marley C.

* * *

"Given the nature of employment, motherhood, participation in a family unit, and socializtion with friends, I would venture to say that I receive as many USSs as I deliver. . . . The balance of the two must be fairly even because I cannot honestly say that I am not overburdened by suggestions from others, nor do I feel compelled to 'give my two cents' too often without invitation." -- Kathy D.

* * *

"I have learned to cut waaaay back on USSs. I used to be a 90/10 give-to-take person. I believe I am under 50/50 now. And I try to wait until asked, but old habits die hard." -- Carl E.

* * *

"My USS ratio (deliver/receiver) is pretty high. Maybe 80/20. My position (as exalted public servant) almost requires me to give advice, while shielding me from others telling me what to do (though, they're undoubtedly talking behind my back, giving very explicit advice!)

"In fairness to myself, I do find I ask, "Do you know what you're going to do, or how you'll handle___.' This question will precede an offer of a USS ('Would you like a recommendation?') and those who know me may accept the USS or they may refuse. . . . But I do give 'em a lot!" -- Nat E.

Rule #11
Listen

*"The best way to persuade people is with
your ears -- by listening to them."*
                              -- Dean Rusk

First, a short quiz.

Q1: How many words a minute does the average person speak?

a) 50   b) 75   c) 100   d) 125   e) 150

*"The older I grow, the
more I listen to people
who don't talk much."*
              -- Germain G. Glien

Q2: How many words a minute can the
human brain process?

a) 100   b) 200   c) 300   d) 400   e) 500

Q3: When you were in school (grades K-12),
what percentage of time did you spend learning
each of the four communication skills?

Reading _____%
Writing _____%
Speaking _____%
Listening _____%
TOTAL   100%

It's a biological fact: our brains have an enormous
capacity to listen. Linguists maintain that the average
human being speaks at a rate of 125 words a minute
but is capable of processing up to 500 words a minute.

Why, then, aren't we better listeners?

To be fair, listening isn't the only thing that we're doing when a human being speaks to us. Our mind is busy deciphering (words and phrases), evaluating (what the person has to say), preparing (how to respond) and daydreaming (in response to visual, auditory and emotional cues). Nonetheless, with a biological gap of 375 words per minute, there seems to be plenty of mental room to decipher, evaluate, prepare, daydream *and* listen. Why then aren't we better?

Listening 101

The answer may lie in educational priorities. The simple truth is that we, as a culture, devote precious little time to listening. Instead, attention and praise are lavished on its more heralded communication siblings -- reading and writing. Few would argue for a diminution of attention to these skills, because they are critical as well. But which communication skill do we use the most? Listening, of course. So why not spend a couple of minutes, now and again, teaching our kids how to improve this skill?

World renowned author M. Scott Peck wonders too, as expressed in his widely acclaimed *The Road Less Traveled*:

> *"We spend an enormous amount of time listening, most of which we waste, because on the whole most of us listen very poorly. An industrial psychologist once pointed out to me that the amount of time we devote to teaching certain subjects to our children in school is inversely proportional to the frequency with which the children will make use of the subject when they grow up. Thus a business executive will spend roughly an hour of his day reading, two hours talking and eight hours listening. Yet in school we spend a large amount of time teaching children how*

"The greatest gift you can give another is the purity of your attention."

-- Richard Moss

"Let others confide in you. It may not help you, but it surely will help them."

-- Roger G. Imhoff

Any Books on Listening?

On a recent trip to the bookstore I asked the information clerk: "Excuse me, where might I find some books on listening?" She looked puzzled and, after pausing for more than a moment, said, "Frankly, I don't know. Let me check with some others and get right back to you." Imagine how differently she might have reacted had I asked her for some books on writing.

to read, a very small amount of time teaching them how to speak, and usually no time at all teaching them how to listen. I do not believe it would be a good thing to make what we teach in school exactly proportional to what we do after school, but I do think we would be wise to give our children some instruction in the process of listening -- not so that listening can be made easy but rather that they will understand how difficult it is to listen well."

"True listening, total concentration on the other, is always a manifestation of love."
-- M. Scott Peck

The Key to All Relationships

Listening is among life's most precious skills because it's the lifeblood of all relationships. From time to time, our daughters will share that they wish to raise their children in the same manner in which Roe and I have raised them (they usually share this, mind you, when they're asking for money or a curfew extension). We tell them that parenting is simple, and boils down to two simple words -- listening and love.

"When I am getting ready to reason with a man, I spend one-third of my time thinking about myself and what I am going to say and two-thirds about him and what he is going to say."
-- Abraham Lincoln

To me, being a good parent means listening to your child, it means listening long enough to hear not just their words, but their meaning. It means listening with your eyes as well as your ears, and keeping your lips pursed long enough to let them have their moment, or perhaps two or three moments. Goodness knows, we'll have our moment soon enough. The fact is, the longer we can resist the temptation to comment, suggest or control, the more we'll learn about our children, *and ourselves.*

Naturally, the benefits of listening extend well beyond parenting; listening nourishes marriages and strengthens friendships, helps build profitable businesses and creates vibrant corporate teams.

The benefits are boundless, which is why Rule 11 urges us to listen with desire and intent, with heart and soul. When we listen -- truly listen -- to our spouse, our children, our friends, our parents, our siblings, our elders, our youth and our peers -- we weave the fabric of life itself.

How do we become expert listeners? Explains Donald L. Kirkpatrick of Kirkpatrick Partners:

"Every person I work with knows something better than me. My job is to listen long enough to find it and use it."
-- Jack Nichols

"Improved listening skills will not necessarily result in improved listening. We must apply these skills. We must be convinced that it pays to listen. The combination of desire (I want to listen), effort (I'm going to work at it), and skill (I know how to do it) will result in improved listening."

The Choice Is Yours

To Kirkpatrick's triad of desire, effort and skill, I offer a fourth -- *awareness*. Before we can improve our ability to listen we must acknowledge that listening is a choice, that every time we decide to speak, we *choose* to stop listening. The concept sounds so simple, yet it stands at the threshold of every human interaction. Naturally, there are times when we try to do both, though our attempts are often cut short by a brusque word from the teacher, as in: *"Mr. Feinberg, if you're talking to Ms. Trumbolt, you're not listening to me."*

How much choice do we have?

If you asked a dozen friends how much choice they have, about what to think or how to feel, you'd engender a dozen opinions. But when we talk about listening, the case is clear -- listening is a choice, plain and simple.

To be honest, knowing that I have a choice -- in every interaction, in every situation -- is more than a little confronting. Knowing that I have a choice makes it more difficult to tell myself: "I just had to tell her how I felt," or "I just had to tell him what was on my mind." When a family member, or close friend, says something that I find objectionable, I can *choose* to say little, or nothing at all. In short, the choice exists. The sad part is, for more years than I care to recount, I never knew the choice was mine.

"As friends, we don't see eye to eye, but then we don't hear ear to ear either."

-- Buster Keaton

So remember:

- When you hear something that upsets you -- choose to listen.

- When you hear something that you object to -- choose to listen.

- When you hear something that you find terribly illogical -- choose to listen.

And remember, by choosing to listen, *you're not waiving your right to speak.* No, you're just choosing not to speak at that specific moment. Later, when the listening is over, after you've told the other person that you need time to reflect (*"I need to think about what you just told me"*), there will be plenty of time to speak. Promise.

Final note: listening may not be the easiest skill to improve, but it just might be the most valuable.

More on listening:
- *Appendix E: "How Good a Listener Are You?" (p200)*
- *Appendix F: "The Human Translator" (page 205)*
- *Appendix G: "Will You Please Just Listen?" (p207)*

Challenge 11A
Lend An Ear

Please find a tip that works for you, and lend an ear.*

Tip #1: Listen non-judgmentally

Tip #2: Attempt to identify the underlying feelings (*"It sounds like you felt disappointed . . ."* and *"How did you feel when . . ."*).

Tip #3: Listen with empathy; focus on feelings.

Tip #4: Show understanding and connection (*"I understand,"* *"I see,"* *"I know how you feel,"* and *"I have felt that way, too"*).

Tip #5: Clarify and paraphrase, particularly the feelings (*"So, you really felt insulted, is that it?"*).

Tip #6: Don't judge with your body language or facial expressions.

Tip #7: Don't show disapproval.

Tip #8: Don't spend your time "preparing your response."

Tip #9: Don't interrupt, evaluate or jump to conclusions.

Tip #10: Use eye contact.

Tip #11: Show interest by nodding, "uh huhs", etc.

Tip #12: Allow long pauses before asking questions, be patient.

Tip #13: Give your full attention, stop other tasks.

Tip #14: Avoid "scene" stealing, advising, interrogating, "sending solutions," correcting, debating.

Tip #15: Remember that listening to either a child or adult helps them feel heard, understood, important, valued, respected and cared about.

*tips were drawn from http://eqi.org/listen.htm

> **The Author's Friends Share Their Thoughts**
> *In a bid to learn how others think, the author assembled a panel of 30 friends (psychologists and social workers among them) to answer some of life's most penetrating questions. Excerpts of their answers appear below.*

The author asked his friends:
How important is listening?

"I took a course on 'Effective Listening Skills' when I was at [work] and the one item that stuck with all the people who took the course was that people are listening at different levels of attention. It became a joke in meetings when someone would become distracted or wasn't paying attention to let them know that they were listening at a different level. The course had some good skills, but over time people didn't use them in the normal course of business. . . . I thoroughly agree with the observation that skills are taught in a direct inverse proportion to how much we use them. . . ."-- Dan V.

* * *

"I definitely agree that listening is a skill, and I think, an acquired one. And indeed, I've never heard of a course in 'Listening 101.' Personally, I'm a very poor listener and most of the time I forget that I am. This lack of listening ability may account for my observation that people seldom really answer a question. For example, 'How far is it?' 'Not far.' " -- Ron T.

* * *

"In my new job I manage 25 salesmen. I have spent time with each of them. Every one of them thinks that their job is to say something to the customer that will make them buy. When I asked each of them, privately, to tell me about one time that they were able

to learn something that would allow them to solve a customer's problem, not one of them could and most didn't know what I was talking about." -- Bruce J.

* * *

"I know little about teaching listening skills, but . . . it seems to me that listening is half conversing. The other half is response -- are you awake? Alive? So . . . the trick has got to be to get everyone involved in the conversation and everyone has to listen and respond to everyone else all the time. In computer systems, the feedback is called an interrupt, and if the computer must complete its operation before it can be interrupted -- vs. somebody just pulled the plug -- it is called a delayed interrupt. A variation of this is used with group response systems, where folks use computers to respond to one another and the group. Two or more people can respond at the same time, but it doesn't interrupt anyone.

"Listening skills are useful, but without the ability to respond, where are we going? A test is one way to get a response, but by the time the test is given, the opportunity for meaningful dialogue is lost. Note taking keeps you busy and may help in studying for a test, but it detracts from engagement with the speaker. All I know how to do is listen, demonstrate to the speaker that I understand (or not) -- usually by rephrasing what I heard and/or asking questions, and listen again."-- Carl E.

Gold
"If speaking is silver, then listening is gold."

         -- Turkish proverb

Easy Listening
"Easy listening exists only on the radio."
         -- David Barkan

Unfold and Expand
"Listening is a magnetic and strange thing, a creative force. The friends who listen to us are the ones we move toward. When we are listened to, it creates us, makes us unfold and expand."

         -- Karl Menninger

Where Discipline Problems Begin
"It has been said that 90% percent of discipline problems come from children wanting adults to listen to them. One study reported that the number one request from suicidal teenagers was for adults to listen to them, because it is the ultimate expression of how much effort and energy we wish to invest in other people."

         -- http:eqi.org/listen.htm

Rule #12
Be Kind to Others

"Kindness is the golden chain by which
society is bound together."
                    -- Johann Wolfgang Von Goethe

If you made a list of the human qualities that you admire most, you would probably rank human kindness near the top. Yet, day to day, and moment to moment, we act in ways that are cruel, we speak in ways that are harsh.

Why is that? Why do we so often fail to measure up? Why do we choose to take steps that are unkind?

Rule 1 urges us to "be kind" to the most important person in the world, and Rule 12 urges us to consider the other seven billion. Not that we're likely to meet many of them. Think about that. Think about how few of the world's travelers you'll meet face to face. Is it too much to ask that we treat those few we encounter with an extra bit of kindness?

"Kindness has converted more sinners than zeal, eloquence or learning."
    -- Frederick W. Faber

Human kindness ranks among the world's most precious resources because a kind word, a soothing touch, a playful smile, can do more to lift up the human psyche than a car full of CDs, a closet full of sweaters, or a bank account full of zeros.

Rule 12 urges us to exhibit kindness in *every* encounter. It encourages us to adopt kindness as a lifestyle, as a way of interacting with each member of the human race, not to mention our sisters and brothers from the animal kingdom.

Rule 12 tells us what to do . . .

> *. . . hold doors . . . smile at strangers . . .say please (and thank you) . . . yield to those in a hurry (at the grocery store or in ticket lines) . . . praise others . . . compliment friends . . . buy gifts for family members (when it's <u>not</u> their birthday) . . . send flowers and cookies to elderly neighbors.*

. . . and what not to do . . .

> *"Kind words do not cost much. Yet they accomplish much."*
> *-- Blaise Pascal*

> *. . . avoid being harsh with telemarketers (they're just trying to earn a living) . . . don't be curt with the store manager, even when they're at fault . . . don't speak ill of others, though they may have disappointed you.*

Taking Every Opportunity

Of course, *being kind* is just half the battle; the more dynamic challenge is to promote kindness at every opportunity, that is, to let others know that, no matter the circumstance, they always can *choose* to deliver a kind word, in a gentle manner.

Of course, telling someone that they're being unkind can, in and of itself, be unkind -- so it's a tricky and delicate proposition. But I keep trying. When I watch my daughters verbally spare I'll often try to lightly interject (sometimes, not so lightly), something simple, along the lines of: "Hey, don't forget Rule 12." My daughters know the meaning of the rule and, even though they may choose to continue, the message often resonates.

Adopting Kindness As a Lifestyle

Some years ago my sister Ilene crafted a beautiful piece on adopting kindness as a lifestyle. The occasion was a special project in which Bar and Bat Mitvah students were asked to record daily "acts of kindness." Ilene offered these candidates:

♦ Calling a sick friend to see how they are feeling;
♦ Saying thank you to the person who drove you somewhere;
♦ Telling a friend how good they look;
♦ Inviting someone to a party, not because you want to, but because you know that they'll feel badly if they're not invited;
♦ Raising money for a worthy cause; and
♦ Helping someone, without being asked.

Ilene's final word to these young adults: "What we hope you will learn, as you become an adult, is that by being kind and helping others, you not only will be giving of yourself, you'll make yourself feel good as well."

How Much Time Do You Spend In "Regret Cycle?"

Think back to a time when you acted unkindly -- perhaps you raised your voice or simply raised an eyebrow. Perhaps it was an act of omission -- neglecting to buy a birthday present or choosing to rush along while a woman struggled with her crutches.

The pattern is familiar to us all -- we take an ill-suited action and, in the moments that follow, we begin to justify the action. Soon our justification turns to regret, and we begin re-playing the incident, wishing we had taken a different path and made a better choice. When regret rears its head, as it always does, we enter the realm of PRC, our "Personal Regret Cycle."

"Kindness consists in loving people more than they deserve."
-- Jacqueline Schiff

Like a closed loop tape that plays without end, our PRC recalls the incident, first every five minutes (then later, perhaps every 10), and soon regret turns to shame, and the wish to start anew. Over the course of a day, no less a lifetime, imagine how many hours we spent "regretting," wishing we had chosen different words, or voiced a softer tone.

So . . .

. . . the next time someone cuts you off in traffic,

. . . the next time your doctor makes you wait,

. . . or your spouse lashes out,

. . . or the bank line won't move,

. . . or your child forgets to finish their chores,

"No act of kindness,
no matter how small, is
ever wasted."

-- Aesop

be kind.

Be kind with those who try to help you (flight attendannts, servers, sales clerks) -- even when it appears they're doing anything but;

Be kind with those who are making a living by contacting people (telemarketers, door-to-door salesmen) -- even when it appears that their only purpose in life is to interrupt your dinner;

Be kind with those who try to solve your problems (doctors, car mechanics, plumbers) -- even though you're spending your valuable time and money;

Be kind with your friends, even though they're not always there to listen or support you in ways that you desire;

And above all, be kind with your family, even though, at times, they evoke the strongest emotions that you possess.

The Moments Will Come

Surely, we'll be tested often, for nary a hour goes by without an emotional upset, spurred by anger or frustration, irritation or complacency. These are the moments that challenge us to place a smile in front of a harsh word.

So the next time you hear someone utter an unkind word, or do an unkind deed, take a moment to resolve NOT to follow their example.

Just be kind.

"If someone were to pay you $.10 for every kind word you ever spoke and collect $.05 for every unkind word, would you be rich or poor?"
-- author unknown

Do It Now
"I expect to pass through this world but once. Any good therefore that I can do, or any kindness that I can show to any fellow creature, let me do it now. Let me not defer or neglect it, for I shall not pass this way again."
-- William Penn

Challenge 12A
"Thank you for calling, and best of luck!"

I can think no more incendiary moment that receiving a phone call, during dinner, from a telemarketer. You're tired from a long day's work and you're noshing on your meatloaf and potatoes when the phone rings. On the other end is a salesperson who tells you that you absolutely, positively, have to purchase their credit card.

What do you do?

A) hang up?
B) yell some expletive into the phone, and then hang up?
C) listen for a moment, or two, then try your best to get off the phone before you get all worked up? or
D) thank them for calling and wish them good luck on their evening's calls?

For years, I followed path "C," that is, I'd listen for a moment or two and then, invariably, would become agitated, and sometimes downright hostile. But, over time, I began to think about what the telemarketer must be going through. What was their evening like? After all, they were just trying to make a living. It seemed to me unlikely that their sole purpose in life was to upset me. Why, then, was I so irritated, so unnerved?

So I tried an experiment. I simply decided to stop -- to stop being rude, to stop hanging up, to stop being unkind. Naturally, there were times when the person on the other end was overly aggressive, but for the most part, the callers were cordial and respectful. In short, the experiment worked - both parties left the conversation a touch complete. At least, I know I did.

So the next time a telemarketer calls, be kind. Don't hang up, or get irritated or upset. Thank them for calling, tell them (in the nicest way possible) that they have no chance of making a sale with you tonight, then wish them good luck on their night's calls. Try this just once . . . and you'll know.

The Author's Friends Share Their Thoughts
In a bid to learn how others think, the author assembled a panel of 30 friends (psychologists and social workers among them) to answer some of life's most penetrating questions. Excerpts of their answers appear below.

The author asked his friends:
What kind act have you done lately?

"I had my students write me paragraphs about themselves to get them familiar with saving files and using the printer, but I really like hearing about the kids' lives and hobbies, etc. I was very touched at the personal things kids wrote to me. I am a perfect stranger to almost all of them, but they all wrote personal things besides the usual info. I have four students who have had parents die in the last year and several who have lost parents as youngsters.

"One girl wrote about missing her mother who is in Korea and can't come here to live with them. One girl wrote about not being able to get a parking permit, as a senior, because she was late turning in the form. One boy complained about not having time to get a locker. He is a senior, and they weren't given lockers because there aren't enough. The school figured that seniors could request a locker in writing if they really wanted one, but this young man, who recently is in remission with cancer, has to change into his football gear and be at practice on time or he won't get playing time, etc.

"So, I decided that since my kids were so honest and personal, I would try and help some of them solve their problems. I went to the security officer's office and got a locker for the young man and I got the last available parking space on the campus for the young lady who didn't get a parking space.

"I can't do a lot for the kids without parents

except be kind and gentle and hope they'll let me know if I can do something specific for them. We have a lot of young people under great stress -- some from their own making, but most from conditions they cannot control."
-- Gail C.

* * *

"On Mother's Day I was in the restroom at a fancy hotel, wrapping gifts that were to be presented to [our] loving mothers within minutes. In walked a women with a 6-8 month old child that had a very dirty diaper. She didn't have any of the necessary equipment to change the child except for a new diaper and a wipe or two. Once I noticed what the situation was, I offered to help by supplying her with tissue paper to rest the baby on, as well as wet papertowels with some soapy water. That was what I considered to be a kind gesture towards a total stranger.

"When I think about the kindnesses I offer my family and friends, I notice that most are geared towards [my husband]. The other night I could tell he had a lot on his mind and I randomly offered him a backrub without asking for one in return.

"Although the [two] didn't happen in a day, I thought they may be good examples."
-- Marnie B.

* * *

What kind act have you done lately? *(continued)*

"1. For those I know, I have made myself available as a ride for my children's friends this summer. Today, I gave a ride to a child who needed one and might have had to walk a distance in the heat otherwise.

"2. Smiling and getting smiles back with strangers continues to be one of my small, maybe insignificant or significant kindnesses in the world. I opened a door at the store for a woman with a baby stroller to help her get in more conveniently." -- Bobbi C.

* * *

"I was in the intensely busy Grand Central Subway Station in New York City. I was standing at the turnstile, behind a mother who was holding the hand of one small child and pushing another in a stroller. She let one child go under the turnstile and then tried to swipe her Metrocard so that she and the child in the stroller could go through. After three swipes the card was not working and she started to panic. I took my Metrocard and swiped it for her, and she went through. She went one way and I went another and I never saw her again." -- Ilene F.

* * *

"I have just returned from 2 weeks of business travel and I have been absolutely dumb-struck by the consistent friendliness, yes almost kindness, of people outside of the New York area. People regularly say good morning, always stop their car at the airport cross walk to let me cross, hold doors, smile, say how good the food is at a restaurant . . . and the list goes on.

"I've gotten to wondering whether it's the stress of NY, our bringing up, just the culture or what. The rest of the country is much kinder and I found it makes the day a little nicer. By the way, before long I was doing all these things too and found the re-entry to NYC particularly tough. Included in the itinerary was Freeport (Maine), Seattle, Portland, (Oregon), Dallas and Denver." -- Bruce J.

* * *

"One day in the midst of all the excitement and craziness in the City of Baltimore Police Department, I saw a photocopy taped to one of the office walls. It suggested that if you show you care about a person and address them by their first name, you may get better results.

"So I tried it out several times over the past week or so, and, believe it or not, it works quite well. So well, in fact, that this combined with a smile has become a standard operating procedure in successfully conducting business with people from all walks of life." -- Dave R.

Rule #13
Help Others

"There are two ways of spreading light: to be the candle or the mirror that reflects it."
-- Edith Wharton

When was the last time you helped someone?

Perhaps you picked up a friend's prescription at the drug store, called the doctor's office for your mother or just listened to someone who needed to talk. Or perhaps you cooked a meal for a sick neighbor, stopped your car to let a stranger walk by, or helped a friend move furniture into their new apartment.

There are few actions in life more noble than helping another human being. Yet, in our daily struggle to survive, we often neglect to reach out and *help* someone.

"Nothing that I can do will change the structure of the universe. But maybe, by raising my voice, I can help the greatest of all causes -- goodwill among men and peace on earth."
-- Albert Einstein

Rule 13 urges us to move beyond the passive steps (respecting "Personal Preference Items" (PPIs), avoiding "Unsolicited Suggestions" (USSs)) and take *positive* steps to help our fellow travelers.

When we carry a friend's mattress up a long flight of stairs, we help physically, and when we listen to a friend struggle through a difficult time, we help emotionally. We help in ways large (e.g., building a shelter for the homeless) and small (e.g., helping a child study for a science test); we help when the medical stakes are high (dialing 911) and low (sitting bedside, stroking a young one's head while they recover from a fever). Certainly, we help. But we can do more.

Take a moment, if you please, to read through the following questions, each of which highlights a *helping* verb. As you read through the list, try to visualize a person that you have helped in this way. I promise that the exercise, which will take but a few minutes, will be illuminating.

In the last year . . .

. . . who have you encouraged?

. . . who have you guided?

. . . who have you supported?

. . . to whom have you extended a courtesy?

"The most satisfying thing in life is to have been able to give a large part of oneself to others."

-- Pierre Teilhard de Chardin

As we strive to match faces to verbs, I urge you to do the same exercise with these "negative" verbs.

In the last year . . .

. . . who have you criticized?

. . . who have you chastised?

. . . who have you reprimanded?

. . . who have you judged?

Sadly, we often find it easier to recall the criticism than the compliment.

Human beings are quick to respond to life emergencies. In these situations, we don't *think* about helping, we just act. And, when people cry out for help -- for physical or emotional support -- we are eager to respond. But Rule 13 is not simply about responding to crises, or calls for help, it's about helping others in the rest of

---

Challenge 13A
The Red Light Challenge

The next time you find yourself waiting for the red light to change, ask yourself:

"Who have I helped today?"

If your mental search yields a pleasing result, take a moment to smile, inwardly. If your search comes up short, decide to help someone -- anyone -- before you go to bed this evening.

It'll make for more pleasant dreams.

---

life's moments -- you know, that other 99.9%.

Rule 13 is about *taking the initiative,* about finding ways to help family members and friends, and even strangers. It's about bringing bagels to work or fixing your parents' faucet; it's about smiling to an elder or helping a stranded driver; about hugging your child or holding the elevator, loading groceries for a neighbor, cooking dinner for your family, offering kind words to the checkout clerk, letting drivers enter your traffic lane or just listening to a friend share their day's travails.

"The more credit you give away, the more will come back to you. The more you help others, the more they will want to help you."
-- Brian Tracy

From the moment the sun rises, until long after it sets, they'll be plenty of opportunities to use Rule 13.

Grab one.

The author asked his friends:

What's the difference between 'being kind' and 'helping others'?

"Seems to me that 'helping others' is a positive action, a concrete step you take to aid another individual. 'Being kind,' I think, can be a lifestyle. I know a lot of folks who are great at 'helping others' but who aren't kind people: they scream at underlings, abuse nameless/faceless service folks, and are generally nasty to anyone they perceive to be beneath them." -- Joe B.

* * *

"Just a thought about the difference between 'being kind' and 'helping others' . . . I think PART of being kind is helping others, but it's not inclusive. One can be kind by saying kind words, showing respect for others in many ways, listening, etc. Helping others is part but not all of being kind." -- Marley C.

True Giving
"You give but little when you give of your possessions. It is when you give of yourself that you truly give."
-- Kahlil Gibran

Rule #14

Listen to Your Heart

*"Once you make a decison, the universe
conspires to make it happen."*
                    -- Ralph Waldo Emerson

Let's face it, you're a decision-making machine.

Should I look for a new job?

*Should I buy the chunky peanut butter or
the plain?*

Should I put more money into the stock market?

Should I continue reading this book?

Should I stay in the relationship?

*Should I make hamburger casserole for dinner,
or order Chinese? (hmmm, I'll go for Chinese)*

*"Make decisions from
the heart and use your
head to make it work
out."*
                    -- Sir Girad

Today, again, you'll make more than 25,000 decisions, more than 700 million in a lifetime. Granted, the vast majority are *autonomic* or *involuntary* -- moving your eyes to read the words on this page, moving your hand to bring the drink to your lips, shifting positions in your easy chair.

Autonomic decisions are said to carry more than 95% of our decision-making load; but even at 5%, that means we make a thousand "conscious" decisions every day.

And you thought you weren't good at making decisions.

The self-help literature is replete with strategies for improving our ability to make decisions. Each author proposes unique characteristics, proprietary step-by-step formulas, and cautionary footnotes that highlight the pitfalls and perils. But, fundamentally, the steps are all the same -- 1. define the problem; 2. propose solutions; 3. gather data; 4. analyze the data; 5. select a solution; and 6. reexamine as needed.

"That should be considered long which can be decided but once."
-- Publilius Syrus

Rule 14 proposes a simple formula -- some might call it a biological bypass -- a decision-making strategy to rouse a part of our system that too often lies dormant. The formula is simple, and relies on instincts and intuition:

Step 1 -- Quiet your mind

Step 2 -- Listen to your heart

Should I invite them to dinner?

Should we look for a new place to live?

Should I ask for a raise?

Should I start doing the bills or finish cleaning the kitchen?

One night our teenage daughter Olivia was struggling to decide between two Friday night invitations -- one to a high school football game with close friends, the other to a party with new faces. Soft commitments had been made to each, making the decision ever more delicate. Olivia began to formally contemplate the pros and cons (a popular step) when I asked her what she *really* wanted to do, what her heart said. She paused, looked inside and quickly found her decision. Her heart knew.

How Robust Is Your PDM*?

In the working world, corporate executives attend seminars to "learn" how to make better decisions, on the bet that a more educated decision-maker will increase their firm's bottom line. But in our personal lives, no comparable training exists (strangely, two of life's most frequently used skills -- listening and decision-making -- are never formally taught in school). Instead, we're left to shape our PDM by a series of trials and errors. We build our PDMs by observing the decision-making styles of our parents, our peers and our leaders; but in the end, we're left to fend for ourselves, with no visible guidelines or fenceposts.

"All our final decisions are made in a state of mind that is not going to last."

-- Marcel Proust

Compounding the problem, we rarely let our engines idle long enough to take a good look at the parts, or inspect the construction. If we did, we'd see how vulnerable we are to society's urgings -- we'd see that we build our PDMs for speed, on the false notion that a swift decision-maker is a smart decisionmaker. Nonsense.

A PDM based solely on speed is flawed because it fails to acknowledge this simple fact: all decisions are not created equal. Some are of enormous import, others but a trifling. A healthy PDM must be flexible, capable of adjusting its tempo and style to the gravity of the decision -- from the inconsequential (*should I watch reruns of Seinfeld?*), to the light fare (*where should we go to dinner tonight?*) to the serious (*should I have surgery next month?*).

A healthy PDM relies on a blend of intuition, insight, common sense and wisdom. Too often, we neglect these elements. Having said that, it's important to realize

* your Personal Decision-Making Machine

When Upgrading Your PDM . . .

Whether you're reconstructing your PDM (Personal Decision-Making Machine), or simply doing some light maintenance, here are some guidelines to remember:

- ◆ Remember to resolve distressing feelings first, before making a decision;
- ◆ Remember that each decision is unique and demands a different length of time to make;
- ◆ Try looking into the future to imagine how your heart will feel about a pending decision.

---

that *listening to your heart* is not the same as *seeking personal gratification*. The difference between these two may be as simple as asking:

What's the best use of my time right now?
vs.
What do I feel like doing?

"Most of our executives make very sound decisions. The trouble is many of them have turned out not to have been right."
-- Donald Bullock

Naturally, at times, these questions are intertwined, but an answer from the heart has more to do with embracing responsibility and commitment than it does with seeking personal gratification.

Two examples spring to mind:

Example #1 -- It's late Saturday morning and you're busy at home, working with your children and tending to the chores. As lunch time nears you begin to entertain thoughts of a family outing -- perhaps to lunch, then out to the country. Suddenly the phone rings and your boss, in an easy but unrelenting manner, asks you to stop by "for a few hours" to discuss next week's product launch. What should you do?

Example # 2 -- You have just learned about the death of a friend's parent, a friend you haven't seen in more than three years. The funeral is set for Friday, about a 60 minute drive from your home, and you're deciding whether to attend. Your week has been torrid and, in truth, you were really looking forward to a softly paced Friday afternoon. You try to talk yourself into skipping the funeral -- after all, you haven't seen your friend in three years, the funeral is a long way off, and no one is really expecting you to be there. What should you do?

The answer, in both cases? Listen to your heart. It knows.

Today, again, you'll face a torrent of decisions, you'll face . . .

   . . . difficult decisions, over family and finance;

   . . . complex decisions, over parents and health care;

   . . . challenging decisions, over work and relationships.

At times, the decision load will be overwhelming, the challenges daunting. But if you take a moment to listen to your heart, to its smooth and measured beat, you'll find a pathway free of clutter, and debris.

You'll find that the heart . . . truly knows.

"Whenever I make a bum decision, I go out and make another one."
-- Harry S. Truman

A thought, plus challenge 14A
There's No Such Thing as a Bad Decision

Consider this familiar example. You're heading home from a long day at work when you spot the traffic slowing down up ahead. No stranger to *this* scene, you begin to weigh your options: "Do I stay put and hope that it opens up or do I take the alternate route?" With less than 30 seconds to decide, you quickly evaluate the current data (the mind-numbing traffic in front of you) against historical patterns (those memorable prior commutes). Now, less than a hundred yards from the turn off, you have to decide. You take the alternate route.

Sure enough, less than half a mile up the road, the dreaded tail lights appear and traffic is backing up faster than you can say, "N-I-G-H-T-M-A-R-E." You've barely finished downshifting when your inside voice blurts out: "That was a bad decision."

The Case of the Tired Commuter

I beg to differ. I believe that your decision, by any measure, was a reasonable one -- after all, you evaluated all of the available data (scant as it may have been) and compared it against prior experiences. Let's face it, you had no idea what traffic would be like if you stayed your course. In this specific case ("The Case of the Tired Commuter"), you'll never know which route would have brought you home more quickly.

So why are you beating yourself up? Well?

There are times, of course, when the inverse holds true, when our *reasonable* decisions lead to *positive* results. In these uplifting moments we're tempted to say: "Wow, what a great decision." Resist the temptation. In its place, simply acknowledge that you've made another reasonable decision which, in this particular case, just happened to produce a good result.

The label that we assign to our decisions ("that was a good decision," "that was a bad decision") is more than mere semantics -- it directly affects our ability to grow. When we criticize our decision-making ability we chip away at our self-confidence and self-esteem. Conversely, when we embrace the notion that sound decisions sometimes lead to bad outcomes, we allow ourselves to focus on what matters most -- improving our ability to make ever-more-reasonable decisions.

Separating performance . . . from outcome

One can easily argue that *all* decisions are reasonable, and such an argument might run like this: each time that we render a decision, we're harnessing our available resources -- that is, we're processing data through our brain's logic and emotional centers. And though our system isn't always optimized -- often slowed by fatigue and stress -- we're certainly doing the best that we can, given our system's limitations and our access to relevant data. So it's possible -- just possible -- that *whatever* decision we reach is truly the most reasonable that could have evolved. Obviously, our decisions can have favorable or unfavorable outcomes, *but the quality of our decision need not be dependent on the outcome.*

So, instead of focusing on the outcome, why not spend our time analyzing our decision-making process. Why not spend time posing questions like: "What's my current mental state and how will that affect the quality of my decision?" Or, "What criteria am I using to make this decision?" In this spirit, here's a two-part challenge:

Challenge -- Part I
The next time that you say the words, "That was a bad decision," think about whether you honestly believe that the *decision* was flawed. Take a moment to ask yourself:

> 1. How did I feel about the decision at the time that I made it?
> 2. What distinguishes a good decision from a bad one? (i.e., what's my criteria, my basis for distinguishing good from bad?); and
> 3. Can a good decision have a bad result? If so, was it still a good decision?

Challenge -- Part II (Beg to Differ)
And the next time you hear someone say the words: *"That was a bad decision"* . . . beg to differ. Naturally, you should do so cautiously as most people, after they say these words, are not in the best of humor. But when emotions calm, you might find a moment to explore whether the person truly believes that their *decision*, as opposed to the outcome, was wanting.

The Author's Friends Share Their Thoughts
In a bid to learn how others think, the author assembled a panel of 30 friends (psychologists and social workers among them) to answer some of life's most penetrating questions. Excerpts of their answers appear below.

The author asked his friends:

How do you make decisions?

"Try never to make any decision when in state of : (a) anger, (b) love, (c) lust, (d) infatuation, (e) sickness (as in not feeling well enough to rationally think through things), and last but not least, (f) frustration -- back off, cool down, become more rationale in your thought process." -- Mickey F.

* * *

"Too slowly or too quickly. I never have gotten it right. Like most people, my first instinct is usually better than my first instinct reconsidered. Raised in the conservative mid-west, I was acultured to believe that anything that looks too good probably is. Therefor, I overanalyze and am often too timid. When I moved to New York City, I discovered the perfect place for a midwesterner. Decisions were demanded and the action was fast. Folks like me, who were more deliberative, lived on the energy but worked the decision making process to avoid big mistakes. There were just more options." -- Carl E.

* * *

"I spend a great deal of time teaching my students to reflect on what they decide to do in problem solving, program writing and decisions of life (like Saturday night plans). I personally spend a great deal of time reflecting on things and making decisions to improve situations. On a day to day basis, though, I tend to think quickly on my feet and make decisions quickly for myself and others who ask for input on situations." -- Gail C.

Forks
"When you come to a fork in the road, take it."
-- Yogi Berra

Making Decisions Now
"When possible, make the decisions now, even if action is in the future. A reviewed decision usually is better than one reached at the last moment."
-- William B. Given

Rule #15
Take Risks

*"It is better to err on the side of daring
than the side of caution."*
-- Alvin Toffler

Are you a risk taker?

Actually, I hate that question, so I apologize for even asking it. I hate it because it implies that we're all light switches, when we know that we're all dimmers. Throughout our lives, we are told that we're . . .

♦ introverted or extroverted;
♦ happy-go-lucky or serious;
♦ fearful or fearless;
♦ friendly or bellicose;
♦ selfish or selfless;
♦ risk inclined or risk averse.

"The irony is this: If you don't go in, you can't find out."
-- Richard Stine

How pedestrian. We are, of course, each of these; yet, in a rush to simplicity, we adopt false labels, then spend countless hours living our lives *based* on those labels. How distressing.

In real life, of course, we're both introverted and extroverted, both happy-go-lucky and serious, both fearful and fearless -- just rarely at the same time. In real life, we're not just black or white, we're fuchsia and lavender, magenta and beige, crimson and coral. It depends on the day, and our mood, not to mention the state of our love life and our finances.

And so it is with risk. We both *seek* and *avoid*, just rarely at the same time. The notion that only a portion of us are risk-takers is nonsense. Every time that we change our environment, take a new job or learn a new skill, we risk failure. Every time that we start a new relationship, talk about our feelings or host a party, we risk failure and rejection. Every time that we laugh or cry, we risk embarrassment. Still, we continue to laugh and to cry.

Living On The Edge

"As a parent, your job is not to discourage all risk, but to understand the motivation behind it, and encourage your teens to take positive risks in their lives."
-- Leslie Ellis

The notion that risk-taking is reserved for parachute jumpers and commodity traders is, of course, ridiculous. In the course of a day, each of us takes life risks that dwarf those of our highly publicized adventurers. But society's incessant drive for adventure creates a false notion that unless we're living on the edge, we're not a bonafide risk taker. And once we start believing this, we end up taking fewer risks, and in so doing, lose a bit of ourselves.

Rule 15 encourages us to take risks -- to actively, knowingly, pursue them. Not to be reckless, mind you, but to build them into our lives, in a meaningful and thoughtful way.

Listen to Charles S. Sanford Jr., former chairman and CEO of Bankers Trust Corporation:

> *"Successful people understand that risk, properly conceived, is often highly productive rather than something to be avoided. They appreciate that risk is an advantage to be used rather than a pitfall to be skirted. Such people understand that taking calculated risks is quite different from being rash."*

Sanford suggests that we should take a positive view of risk. He explains:

"Risk is commonly thought of as going against the current, taking the hard way against high odds . . . [but] taking risks is accepting the flow of change [in life] and aligning ourselves with it. . . . For those who understand reality, risk is actually the safest way to cope with a changing, uncertain world. . . .

"In a world of constant change, risk is actually a form of safety, because it accepts that world for what it is. Conventional safety is where the danger really lies, because it denies and resists that world."

"Nothing is more difficult, and therefore more precious, than to be able to decide."
-- Napoleon Bonaparte

To experience success, we must experience risk -- the risk of a new relationship or a new job. And *risk* isn't limited to our love life and the workplace -- risk touches every area of our lives, from the risks we face socially (e.g., introducing ourselves to new people, attending a party where few faces are familiar) to the risks we face emotionally (e.g., telling someone that you don't appreciate their negative attitude).

"If doing it is scary, it's a risk. If you're doing it and it should be scary and you don't have the brains to see it, it's not a risk. If someone else is doing it, it's not even close to risky."
-- Carl Eckstein

Going Out On A Limb

Says Schannon Love, on the importance of risk:

"Risks are full of lessons that impact our growth and development, as well as our perceptions. . . . There's nothing more rewarding than having our efforts result in achievement. Though all risks will not be rewarding, we should appreciate the experience and walk away with something positive. . . . Above all, remember that in order to get the best fruit in life, you must be willing to go out on a limb; or you can just sit around and wait until [the fruit] falls off the tree (rotten and spoiled)."

Sadly, many of us, equate risk-taking with fear and

danger --just talk to any parent of a teenager. But even here, during the most vulnerable time in a person's life -- the teenage years -- risk is something to be managed, not avoided. Lynn Ponton, professor of child psychiatry at UCSF, and author of *"The Romance of Risk: Why Teenagers Do the Things They Do,"* says parents must encourage *intelligent* risk-taking for their teenagers. She explains that since challenge and risk are the primary tools used by adolescents to find out who they are, parents need to help them identify the difference between constructive and destructive risks.

"Never tell me the odds."

-- Hans Solo, in Star Wars

Adds Clinical Counsellor Leslie Ellis, MA, RCC:

"The problem is not so much the fact that teens are attracted to risk, but that this desire often leads them into the wrong kinds of risk. If teenagers' natural courage can be channeled into productive kinds of risk-taking, they may feel less of a need to pursue potentially self-destructive risks. Sports and performing arts, for example, offer challenge and risks that are highly positive. Wilderness experiences, such as the outings facilitated by Outward Bound, are also excellent ways for teens to push their limits in constructive ways. . . . "

Three Tips for Building Your Skill

Risk-taking not only expands a person's potential, it brings notable rewards, opportunity and excitement. Knowing this, here are some straightforward tips for improving your ability to take risks.

Tip I: Adopt a Positive Attitude About Risks
Tip II: Become an Intelligent Risk-Taker
Tip III: Find a Practice Arena

Tip I: Adopt a Positive Attitude About Risks

As you strive to improve your ability to take risks,

remember that:

♦ Risks that fail are opportunities to learn;

♦ Risks help you learn what you don't like;
> *"It's never a waste of time to have experienced something you found unpleasant . . . because knowing what you don't like is as important as knowing what you do like."*
> *-- David Turner, owner, Wordscapes Resume Service*

♦ Risks are subjective and personal;
> *"Risk, like beauty, is in the eye of the beholder. [Something that] may seem risky or dangerous from the outside can seem entirely different to the person in its midst. The hidden variable is commitment." -- Daniel Goleman*

♦ Risks that result in failure often are remembered far longer than risks that result in success.
> *"If we succeed in taking a risk, the success is absorbed into our daily practice, routinized and forgotten; but if we are unsuccessful, the failure is remembered and carried over into assumptions about our abilities, our leaders and our safety." -- Kathryn J. Deiss, Content Strategist, Association of College & Research Libraries (www.acrl.org)*

"The greatest risk is in not taking one."
(This is one of our daughter Natalie's favorite quotes, authored when she was a teenager. Of course, when parenting teenagers, this is not exactly the type of world philosophy you want to encourage. But, Natalie, along with her sisters Melyssa and Olivia, seems to be able to distinguish between risks that are worth taking and those that are not. At least we hope so!)

Tip II: Become an Intelligent Risk-Taker

It's important to understand the concept of intelligent risk-taking -- that is, classifying risks based on the opportunity and positive gains that may result (e.g., the difference between applying for a new job and gambling). The financial experts at Contingency Analysis, Inc. explain:

"Institutions can actually reduce their risks simply by researching them. A bank can reduce its credit risk by getting to know its borrowers. A brokerage firm can reduce market risk by being knowledgeable about the markets it operates in."

To become a more intelligent risk-taker, it's critical to know how you currently assess risks, that is, what criteria you use in evaluating them. It's nearly impossible to improve one's style without knowing what that style is.

"Progress always involves risk; you can't steal second base and keep your foot on first."
-- Frederick Wilcox

Tip III: Find a Practice Arena

Naturally, the key to building any skill is practice, but when it comes to risk-taking, "practice" is not as simple as it sounds. That's why we need to create safe havens in which to "practice" risk-taking. Deiss* explains the concept in a work context:

". . . [F]ear and reticence to risk are consequences of the fact that we have, apparently, only one arena in which to take risks: our 'performance arena,' where we actually do the work we are there to do. We feel that what we are engaged in is entirely too important to us to chance failure or the appearance of failure. . . .

"In an area of less competence, risk is required to beget learning and new practices. What is needed to encourage more risk-taking? Where can this activity best take place? If our performance arena calls on us to deliver our work with a fairly consistent and high degree of quality, where will we find the 'practice arena' in which to learn the new behaviors associated

* Deiss, Kathryn J. *"Steal a Base or Stay Safe? Taking Risks to Grow." Association of Research Libraries Bi-Monthly Newsletter #201, December 1998.*

> ### *The Benefits of Taking Risks*
> *A poem, author unknown:*
>
> To Laugh -- is to risk appearing the fool.
> To Weep -- is to risk appearing sentimental.
> To Reach Out for Another -- is to risk involvement.
> To Expose Feelings -- is to risk exposing your true self.
> To Place Your Ideas, Your Dreams Before the Crowd -- is to risk their loss.
> To Love -- is to risk not being loved in return.
> To Live -- is to risk dying.
> To Try -- is to risk failure.

with risk-taking? One answer is to turn to areas of our work that aren't expressly connected to our delivery of service. . . . "

As managers, not to mention spouses, friends, workers and parents, it's important to create environments which encourage risk-taking. Adds Deiss:

"We must form practice or learning arenas that allow people to develop confidence in themselves and in the benefits of temporary puzzlement and discomfort. By doing so, we will create an atmosphere of safe change that allows for innovation, better job results and satisfaction, and, ultimately, a more successful organization."

"One of the reasons mature people stop learning is that they become less and less willing to risk failure."
-- John W. Gardner

In many ways, our culture is consumed by a desire to minimize risk (e.g., health and financial), or avoid it altogether. We assess it, manage it and analyze it, all because we want it to disappear. But perhaps we should simply relax. Perhaps we should recognize that risk is a natural part of our environment and our humanness and, instead of running from it, try to embrace and enjoy it. Perhaps.

Challenge 15A
Oh, Go Ahead . . . Take A Risk

One day this week, perhaps on your way to work, or on the way to the gas station, consciously decide to take a risk.

It need not be momentous, you need not court danger. The "risk" may be as simple as contacting a friend by letter or phone, proposing an idea at the next meeting, or taking a new route to work (for ideas, see the list, below).

Keep it simple, but make it specific. And rejoice in the knowledge that you, and you alone, will decide what risks to take today, and tomorrow.

For Adults

Break your daily routines
Put your TV in a closet for a week
Travel to work by a different route
Try a new restaurant for lunch

Take a walk during lunch break
Talk to, and get to know,
   somebody new
Investigate other opportunities
   for employment

For the Young at Heart

Learn to cook
Perform at a recital
Join a sports team
Join in a talking circle

Go on a scavenger hunt
Change your hair style
Stay up late on a Saturday
Go to overnight camp
Be a volunteer

Tutor a younger kid
Take music lessons
Stay over at a friend's house
Learn to rollerblade
Learn to ski (water or snow)

Ask someone on a date
Babysit
Give a speech
Talk with someone you like,
   but don't know

More on risk:
Appendix H: "Learning How to Take Risks" (p208)

The Author's Friends Share Their Thoughts
In a bid to learn how others think, the author assembled a panel of 30 friends (psychologists and social workers among them) to answer some of life's most penetrating questions. Excerpts of their answers appear below.

The author asked his friends:
How important is it to be a risk-taker?

"Good topic for me right now. Risk-taking is not something that I . . . am usually looking for, but when issues present themselves that I feel strongly about, I will take more risk. I think that I have taken more risks in some areas as I have gotten older, and less in other areas as I have aged. I think through the consequences of the risky behaviors more carefully now. At present, I would [rate myself at] about a '6' on the continuum, with 10 being most risky. Usually, I am probably at about '4,' so I tend to be midline, but [go to] either side depending on the issue. When I was younger, I might have said I was a 3 and a 7. I think this will continue to fluctuate in my life." -- Bobbi C.

* * *

"I wish I had something unique to offer here, but I must fall back on Homer Simpson: 'Taking stupid risks are what make life worth living.' That about sums it up. Risk is doing something even though it might fail. Stupid risk, I guess, is doing something when the reward isn't worth the cost of failure." -- Joe B.

* * *

"The older I get, and I hate to admit that I'm growing older (is that a state of mind, body, both or neither?), I tend to take a narrorwer view on 'taking risks.'

"Would I take risks with money? Yes. Would I take risks with my children's lives? Most likely not, unless it was a 'life and death' alternative, with no choice (e.g., sickness). Would I take risks with my livelihood -- less and less as I get more advanced in age.

"Risks . . . Older & hopefully wiser equates to more calculation to 'taking risks.'. . no? Younger, brasher -- more willing to 'take a risk' without too much worry about the eventual outcome. [Back then, the] thought process was: it can always be fixed or overcome.

"Risks . . . Exhilarating, gets certain juices flowing, brings about a feeling of [mental sharpness . . . . it seems] that risk is a difficult thing to describe. Without it, do [truly great things] ever happen? On occasion, I'm sure, but it's possible that some are brought about by 'the risk taken.'

"Some of our greatest scientific accomplishments were at the expense of 'accident' versus 'planned scientific procedure.' Is risk / chance not part of the overall process that our supreme being put there for us? To go through life without once in a while 'taking a risk,' I believe mankind would still be floundering in the middle ages." -- Mickey F.

* * *

". . . The importance of taking risks depends on the individual. If someone is challenged by taking risks, and they find it

How important is it to be a risk-taker? *(continued)*

fulfilling, then it is very important, however if risk taking creates massive anxiety, then it is probably not as important." -- Marnie B.

* * *

" 'She's definitely a risk-taker' means she is: intelligent, flexible, willing to try new ideas, follow suggestions, follow her heart/mind, OR She's: crazy/reckless/thoughtless, not very intelligent . . . ! It depends on the context and the person involved." -- Marley C.

Risk is essential
"Risk is essential. There is no growth or inspiration in staying within what is safe and comfortable. Once you find out what you do best, why not try something else?"

-- Alex Noble

Rule #16

You're Free to Change Your Mind At Any Time

"Life has got a habit of not standing hitched.
You got to ride it like you find it. You got to change
with it. If a day goes by that you don't change some
of your old notions for new ones, that is just about
like trying to milk a dead cow."

-- Woody Guthrie

Is consistency overrated?

I posed this question to 30 of my friends and the response was deafening, if not outright consistent: "NO!" They insisted, with penetrating conviction, that consistency is a highly valued human trait, rivaling kindness, trustworthiness and honesty.

It's hard to disagree. Let's be honest, if someone turned to you right now and said, "You know, you're a very consistent person," you would probably receive it as a compliment. And while you might have preferred: "You know, you're a very reliable person," or "you're a very honest person," you certainly would not be ashamed to be known as consistent.

"Slumber not in the tents of your fathers. The world is advancing."
-- Guiseppe Mazzini

Yet consistency can be our undoing, an emotional straightjacket that inexplicably binds us to our past. Yes, consistency is of value on the highways and in the kitchen, but when it comes to making decisions, I believe that it's vastly overrated.

Giving Consistency Its Due

Before I begin a virulent defense of my hypothesis -- that consistency binds us into ever-more-narrow ways of thinking -- let us give consistency its due; goodness knows my friends did.

To the question: "Is consistency overrated?" they wrote:

"The search for static security -- in the law and elsewhere -- is misguided. The fact is security can only be achieved through constant change, adapting old ideas that have outlived their usefulness to current facts."
-- William O. Douglas

> *"Consistency lends a much needed stability to our existence; it grounds us; it reduces fear."*
> *-- Vicki Sullivan*

> *"Imagine a world with no consistency. . . . No movement about the world would be possible without traffic laws. How would we know what clothing to wear? There would be no World Cup. There would be no dinner because you couldn't count on the oven to give a constant cooking temp for the roast. And gravity might be off today . . . And the rhythm method would no longer work." -- Nat Emery*

> *"Consistency is important in establishing routines, especially with young children. . . . Consistency provides the strength to deal with inconsistency when it arises. . . . Consistency is important for children in school in that certain expectations, when consistent, help build a community of learners." -- Marley Casagrande*

We strive for consistency in parenting and athletics and we laud consistency in our schools and our financial institutions. From theatre artists to kitchen appliances, we praise all that is consistent. After all, when we set the oven to 350 degrees it's comforting to know that the temperature will reach that level, and stay there.

But in valuing consistency, we sometimes lose sight of its shortcomings, we sometimes forget that it's not the right prescription for *every* ailment. We often fail to differentiate between moments when consistency is essential . . . from moments when it's simply desirable, or clearly superfluous.

Consistency is *essential* when we're talking about human safety (think: airline crews). And consistency is *desirable* when we're talking about service (think: police officers, electricians, dry cleaners).

"When you're finished changing, you're finished."

-- Benjamin Franklin

But consistency is *superfluous* when it comes to personal opinions and decisions. In the cogitative world of thoughts and feelings -- which lays at the heart of all decisions -- we often fall into the trap of believing that consistency, above all, must be preserved.

Does Consistency Bind Freedom?

Enter Rule 16. Rule 16 is an axiom about freedom -- the freedom to change your mind, not once or twice, but *any time, anywhere.* You're free to *feel* differently today than you did a year ago, a month ago, an hour ago, or a moment ago -- about anything, about anyone.

I thought you said you love this house?"
"I've changed my mind. I'd like to look around."

***

"But I thought you didn't like scary movies?"
"I usually don't, but I thought I'd try this one."

***

"I thought you didn't like vegetables?"
"It's true that I haven't eaten them in a while,
but today I've changed my mind."

***

"I thought you didn't invest in the stock market."
"I've changed my thinking."

***

"I thought you didn't want to spend time with him?"
"I've changed my mind."

"I've changed my mind." Four simple words, yet words that lay a pathway to unbridled freedom. But to claim that freedom -- to become a truly liberated decision-maker -- we must shed our need for OC (opinion consistency), DC (decision consistency) and TC (thought consistency).

"Life is made up of millions of moments, but we live only one of those moments at a time. As we begin to change this moment, we begin to change our lives."
-- Trinidad Hunt

Rule 16's message is simple: instead of striving for consistency, strive for flexibility. Instead of clinging to opinions based on "yesteryear," create new opinions that reflect your feelings, today. Inside of basing decisions on a thousand "yesterdays," base decisions on today, on the facts in front of you . . . and the feelings inside of you.

Note: if you do decide to shed the need for OC (opinion consistency) and DC (decision consistency), your life will become immeasurably easier. By releasing your need for consistency, you'll free up a portion of your mental energy, and, in the end, wind up doing far more of what you wish to do, right now. And for those of you who worry that shedding both OC and DC will lead your decisions to become variable and erratic, or wildly haphazard, fear not. They won't. You'll still end up doing what's sensible. I promise.

Consistency, of course, won't be easy to shed. Social scientists insist that human beings have a natural drive for consistency, have something of a cognitive mandate

A Cautionary Note

Freedom to change one's mind does not confer an abdication of responsibility. As tempting as it might be, a decision not to wash the dishes tonight -- after having agreed to do so -- should not be defended with a casual: "Rule 16."

I suppose one could easily defend such a stance, but it would not be in keeping with the rule's intent, which is simply to add flexibility to our decision-making process, not to abandon commitments and covenants.

to make internal peace among competing attitudes, feelings and thoughts. But though consistency may indeed have a biological link, and remains a valuable survival tool, it's not necessarily the ultimate salve.

A Sign of Extraordinary Strength

Our culture currently views "a change in mind" as a weakness -- particularly in the political arena -- an indication that we're not the bold, clear-headed thinker that we wish to be *or think we should be.* That's crazy talk. Changing one's mind is a sign of extraordinary strength, a symbol of freedom, of openness, of flexibility. Let's return to politics, for just a moment. Suppose that our congressman is recommending a host of new laws to battle global warming, and suppose that a new thorough internationally approved panel finds concerns are overstated? Would it not be appropriate for our congressman to "change his mind" based on the new fndings? We're taking in new data all the time - shouldn't our position be based on the current research?

> *"Nobody told me how hard and lonely change is."*
>
> *-- Joan Gilbertson*

Let's face it, we change our mind every moment of our lives -- every time that we create a new thought (*"I think she's angry at me"*) or declare a new preference (*"I'm thinking of buying a Volvo").* If we view our mind as the sum total of our thoughts, beliefs, preferences and opinions, we change our mind (pardon the pun) consistently.

Why then, are we so defensive? Why do we feel that we need to justify our new preference? Why are we more comfortable with a "change of heart" than a "change of mind?"

"Interested in going to the café?"

"The longer you stay in one place, the greater your chances of disillusionment."

-- Art Spander

*"I thought you hated that place.
Didn't you tell me that you never wanted to go back there?"*

*"Yes, but I just read a piece about the new owner.
Maybe we should give it another try."*

or

*"I'm thinking about buying a foreign car.
What do you think?"*

"You can't be serious. You've been telling me for the last 10 years that there's no chance you'll ever own one. I don't get it."

"Everyone I've talked to lately has had good luck with the imports. They seem to love 'em. Maybe it's time for a change."

A change of mind.

I'm guessing that if you and I sat down together and composed a list of elements that affect how we feel and think at any given moment, we could easily come up with more than 20. Yet, aware of the vicissitudes in human thought, we somehow expect that our feelings, our thoughts, and our decisions should conform to those made in our past. How unrealistic.

In the real world, when we *do* make a change, we

spend an enormous amount of time justifying it. We cite new data (*"I just read an article"*) or a new source (*"I've been talking to some friends"*). But wouldn't it be nice, just once, if we didn't feel compelled to justify every change? Wouldn't it be nice, just once, to simply state our preference without having to explain why?

I remember invoking Rule 16 some years ago during an overly noisy basketball practice. I was coaching a team with a dozen 13 year old girls, so it always was a touch noisy (let's just call it "social"). In a bid to get them to focus, I sometimes ran drills in silence, but this evening I planned to let them chat. Then, moments before the drill commenced, I blurted out: "Let's run it in silence." Amanda looked up and said, "But Mr. Ferber, you said we could talk." To which I replied: "Rule 16."

Any Time, Anywhere

"Don't fear change -- embrace it."
-- Anthony J. D'Angelo

Rule 16 says you're free to change your mind *at any time,* free to return to the department store that you so harshly criticized without having a reason. You're just free. You don't need to rely on a friend's positive experience or a favorable article in the local paper. You're simply free.

But remember, if you choose to publicly unveil these liberties, fellow travelers -- particularly those for whom "consistency" is a highly valued trait -- will challenge your new-found freedom and resist, or worse, attack. You'll be told, straight out: "You can't just change your mind like that."

To which you can simply respond: **"Rule 16."**

Be sure to smile when you say it.

The Author's Friends Share Their Thoughts
In a bid to learn how others think, the author assembled a panel of 30 friends (psychologists and social workers among them) to answer some of life's most penetrating questions. Excerpts of their answers appear below.

The author asked his friends:
When it comes to making decisions, how important is it to be consistent?

"The idea of consistency should not enter into the [decision-making] process. Sound decisions are based upon . . . the facts and figures [in front of] you, and the past experience one has had with similar facts and figures. Decisions can therefore be based upon direct relationships or analogues. For example, psychological profiling and assessments are based upon questions in a matrix, dependent upon precedent and analogy.

"Decisions are made based upon these tests because the information regarding the psychological assessment is comparatively consistent. A decision is therefore, based upon analogous past experience, not necessarily consistent with past experience." -- Bobbi C.

* * *

"It's not the decision that needs to be consistent as much as the problem-solving involved in reaching it. It goes back to values which drive many decisions and those values need to be consistent, not the decisions per se. For example, your child wants to extend his bedtime one night when he has to get up early the next day for school. You say no, he needs his sleep to function well in school. The next night is Friday and he wants to stay up past his bedtime to visit with Grandma who came for the weekend. He doesn't have any obligations until noon. Yet let him stay up. Was this inconsistent? No, the decisions

were different, but the problem-solving was consistent." -- Marley C.

"You should be consistent when you are talking about moral and ethical imperatives. Everything else is a case-by-case issue. Consistent behavior is valuable -- so long as it does not inhibit creativity." -- Joe B.

* * *

"I believe I am willing to change my mind in the face of superior logic or an unanticipated outcome resulting from a mistake in judgment. Now that I am old and wise I consistently try to avoid making statements or commitments that will lead to these situations." -- Carl E.

* * *

"Strikes me as interesting [to consider if] consistency -- when pursued without judgment or consideration -- becomes rote, mindless or thoughtless. Or how often is mindlessness, thoughtlessness and rote decision-making confused with consistency?

"I think I try to be consistent in my process of evaluating incoming data and how I want/ need to act as a result. I know I work very hard not to allow myself to be trapped into reacting in a pre- determined way. That kind of process is what has prevented me from being able to change." -- Bruce J.

The author asked his friends:
Is consistency overrated?

"Consistency is overrated, highly valued and impossible. What is McDonalds, if not consistent? Almost consistent and bad for you. What is an amusement park the second day? Not as amusing. Ever work on an assembly line? I did -- and quit.

"On a personal level, the trick is trying to deliver a consistent message through your words and actions to your kids. Tough job." -- Carl E.

* * *

"We always hear how it is important to be consistent with kids. I agree with that, even though I find it hard. I think that kids do feel more comfortable when they can count on consistent responses.

"However, I think that it is a mistake to stay with a position, just for the sake of consistency, when it becomes clear that a change might be good. I think the rule might be that it's good to be consistent, as long as it doesn't make you inflexible." -- Ilene F.

* * *

"In everyday life, consistency is good, [but] it may be overrated . . .

"After recently changing my work environment from a rural environment to a city environment, I have been exposed to many people and many different kinds of people. Working in the city you see many people who consistently do the same thing day in and day out. These are for the most part poor people. They consistently beg at the same corner. One lady (dressed nicely) consistently sits in the same park bench and carries on conversations with herself. She argues with herself. There appears to be two sides to her. She doesn't acknowledge anyone else's presence. As one friend recently remarked in today's terms -- wouldn't it be interesting to download her hard drive and see what it reads? These are extreme examples of where consistency is not good. It may be safe for some people, but it also may be detrimental to one's own health and welfare.

"A change in environment (not being consistent) would be good for these folks. Perhaps that is what the doctor would order . . . Change, though hectic, makes life more interesting!" -- Dave R.

* * *

"I assoicate consistency with quiet, calm behavior that comes from thoughtful human beings who think before they speak and don't shout out the obvious. To me it is the opposite of erratic berhavior.

"The world we live in is a far different one from when I grew up [the 1930s-1940s] and even from [the 1960s-1970s]. I could say that also about the early years of my grandchildren.

"*Future Shock* pointed out the problem years ago: the rapid advances in communication and science, the speed in transportation, the mobility of people, the dislocation of lives due to wars, autocratic regimes, divorces in so-called stable environments. In *Future Shock*, Toeffler pointed out that more inventions and changes had taken place in the five prior years than in all the time man has been on earth.

"And yet, those observations pale when compared to the technological advances in communication and the development of Internet information and commerce in the last

139

Q: Is consistency overrated? (continued)

five years.

"Bewildering times. Information overload. All cry out for some consistency in human behavior and some easily recognized patterns of conduct that are not buffeted by high-speed changes happening all around us. The loudness of radios in passing cars and the high frequency emissions from TV and movies plus the explosion in chat rooms suggest that every one is shouting to be heard and not too many people are listening. Communication and behavior are subject to knee jerk responses which don't allow for too much thought.

"The calming effect of consistency would be very welcome in these hectic times." -- Arnold F.

* * *

"A few thoughts on consistency.

"I think we value consistency because it is how we set rules and follow them. In sports particularly we want consistent rules or the game is not fair. However, in other parts of life there are few arenas where we have clear winners and losers and things are not usually black and white. We want our teachers to grade consistently, but of course, they are also encouraged to make exceptions, and often look beyond the test to consider other things in giving the overall grade. One of the reasons we are inundated with lawyers is that the laws are constantly being interpreted and are not followed and applied consistently. When we have tried to add some consistency, such as mandatory sentencing, it often creates other

problems and does not serve the function of 'fairness.' As a parent or in other parts of my personal experience, I think it can be helpful to be consistent, but is not always possible or desirable. This is an issue that comes up in daily life frequently." -- Karin U.

* * *

"As an educator and parent, consistency is very important. As an educator and parent, change is important as well. We all have to get used to inconsistency, but we wouldn't recognize inconsistency unless consistency had prevailed. Art Costa, a highly-respected educator, has identified at least 12 intelligent behaviors, or what we do when an answer is not readily apparent, including: persistence, listening with empathy and understanding, managing impulsivity, working with accuracy and precision, thinking creatively, and flexibility in thinking, etc. Flexibility in thinking is critical in dealing with inconsistency and it's the people who are not flexible thinkers who seem to have the most difficulty with change (and life in general!) of any sort.

". . . Consistency in the workplace is important to accomplish goals, yet inconsistency can be beneficial in providing opportunities as well. I think 'out of the box' thinking, which certainly involves inconsistency, can be productive and fun.

"Different situations require differing levels of consistency. Some flourish with inconsistencies, and others do not (such as meeting basic needs). So, there's a huge 'gray area' with regard to consistency." -- Marley C.

Rule #17
Welcome Mistakes

"If I had to live my life over again,
I'd try to make more mistakes next time."
                    -- Nadine Stair

Mistakes. Are they a blessing or a curse?

Our confusion stems from two paradoxical messages we hear about them:

> ◆ Message #1: Mistakes are evil -- avoid them at all costs.

> ◆ Message #2: Mistakes are one of life's most powerful learning tools. Pursue them.

"Mistakes are the usual bridge between inexperience and wisdom."
                    -- Phyllis Therous

Which are we to believe?

Philosophically, I side with Message #2, but in real life I live by #1 -- I hate making mistakes and I spend far too much time trying to avoid them. In so doing, I miss out on countless opportunities. I wish it weren't so.

Sure, I give lip service to the notion that mistakes speed the learning process, that mistakes force us to learn more quickly and grow more completely. But my emotional system doesn't buy it; my emotional system is inexorably tied to Message #1 -- mistake-avoidance. That's why Rule 17 is of great personal interest.

141

Mistakes, of course, are our constant companions, daily reminders that we are human. Not a day goes by -- sometimes not an hour -- when we don't tell ourselves: "Oooooh, that was a mistake."

-- At times we make high-profile mistakes, the kind that damage our relationships (*"I responded too harshly"*);

-- At times we make modest mistakes, over-commiting our resources, both personal and financial (*"I never should have volunteered for that project,"* or *"We never should have bought that car"*);

"More people would learn from their mistakes if they weren't so busy denying them."
-- Harold J. Smith

-- And at times, far more than we'd like to recount, we make minor mistakes, whether it's tending to our children (*"I'm sorry that I didn't listen to you the first time"*) or our parents (*"I'm sorry that I didn't listen to you the first time"*).

Why Are We So Surprised?

The puzzling part is, since we know that human beings are mistake-making machines, why are we so surprised when we mis-step? Today, again, we'll make dozens of mistakes. Knowing this in advance, why are we so ill-equipped to handle them?

When you signed on as a member of the human race (you recall the signing ceremony, don't you?), you no doubt bought the package deal -- moments of triumph and peace, alongside moments of failure and anxiety. Yet though failure was part of the package deal, we nonetheless spend endless hours working to avoid mistakes. And it takes a toll. Mistake-avoidance consumes an enormous amount of psychic energy, tying up our brain circuitry in ways we know are detrimental. Think back to your last mistake and try to guess how many minutes, if not hours, you spent in "regret cycle?"

Too many.

Rule 17 encourages us to *welcome* mistakes -- not just acknowledge or accept them, but to welcome them. Frankly, it's a daunting notion, particularly to those of us who have spent most of our lives trying to avoid them.

The math is elementary: if you spend one less moment regretting (your mistakes), you'll have one more moment available for learning/ It's a simple formula:

More Mistakes = More Learning

Can you recall a time when you spent hours regretting a mistake? Imagine if you turned this negative energy into a positive force. The professionals at the Medical Center of Central Georgia, in Macon, Georgia, explain how:

> *"A mistake is actually the first step in learning. When trying to learn something that is new to you, the learning comes from making a mistake and correcting it. If you make no mistakes, you don't learn. I like snow skiing and when I take a lesson the instructor usually reminds me, 'If you are not falling, you are not learning.' So mistakes are not bad, they are good. Maybe you should make as many mistakes as you can in order to more quickly learn. The next time that you make a mistake, become excited and say to yourself, 'This is great. I am going to learn something now!' Try this 'rethinking' approach to any problem and your mood and behavior will improve."*

The challenge, of course, is to retrain our thoughts, to create a positive inner dialogue every time we mis-

"If it weren't for all the mistakes I have made, I would not know as much as I do now."
-- Buckminster Fuller

step. Our experts continue:

"A mistake is just an event and there can be many possible reactions to it. The reactions all depend upon what you think the mistake means. What you think the mistake means depends on your rule for mistakes. Many of us learn that a mistake is a bad thing and a sign of failure. Our rule says simply that, 'Mistakes are bad. If you make one then you are bad.'

"This is just one rule. There are other points of view. When my daughter was six years old and trying to learn to ride a bicycle she taught me a different rule. After falling off the bike many times as you do with this learning process, she observed that, 'When you learn to ride a bike you have to start with the falling down.' This was true. Fall off enough and you learn to ride. So, we learn by making mistakes."

How should we regard mistakes? Five choices:

 -- Deny them (option #1)

 -- Acknowledge them (option #2)

 -- Accept them (option #3)

 -- Welcome them (option #4)

 -- Pursue them (option #5)

Personally, I've spent plenty of time exercising option #1, have become comfortable with #2, struggled with #3, contemplated #4 and laughed at #5. Laugh though I might, #5 remains my personal goal, however distant it may seem.

Rule 17 is about moving past the mistake by con-

"A life spent making mistakes is not only more honorable, but more useful than a life spent doing nothing."
-- George Bernard Shaw

"The greatest mistake a man can make is to be afraid of making one."
-- Elbert Hubbard

sciously freezing our regret cycle and directing our thoughts to the present, and then the future. In its purest form, Rule 17 is a curative, helping us learn, not lament, offering delight in place of despair.

Make no mistake: Rule 17 is a pathway to freedom.

5,000 Mistakes
"The sooner you make your first 5,000 mistakes, the sooner you will be able to correct them."
> *-- Kimon Nicolaides*

Making Too Few
"The trouble in America is not that we are making too many mistakes, but that we are making too few."
> *-- Philip Knight*

Challenge 17A
After Your Next Mistake . . .

Try these simple steps, to ease the pain:

> **Step 1** -- Pause and acknowledge the mistake: *"I made a mistake."*

> **Step 2** -- Remind yourself that you're a human being who has many wonderful qualities, one of which is the ability to make mistakes and learn from them: *"I want to learn from my mistakes."*

> **Step 3** -- Try to imagine the next time you're in a similar situation, then think about how you'd like to respond, how you'll learn from your mistake.

All the while, remember that mistakes are one of life's most valuable tools for helping us improve, for helping us become the person we want to become. Don't ignore them, don't try to avoid them, use them wisely.

Challenge 17B
Trim Your "Regret Cycle"

Think back to a recent mistake and ask yourself:

"How persistent was my regret cycle?"

. . . that is, how often did thoughts of regret appear in my mind, in the minutes and hours and days that followed?

Then, the next time you make a mistake, try to cut short your "regret cycle," try to shift your thoughts from "regret" *("I wish I hadn't done that!)* to "growth" (*"what can I take from this experience?"*). By doing so, you'll be spending more time learning and less time mulling.

Try this . . . and you won't regret it!

The Author's Friends Share Their Thoughts
In a bid to learn how others think, the author assembled a panel of 30 friends (psychologists and social workers among them) to answer some of life's most penetrating questions. Excerpts of their answers appear below.

The author asked his friends:
What's the difference between a mistake and a bad decision?

"I think of a mistake as more impulsive than a decision, less carefully thought out. 'Decision' implies that all sides were examined and that a choice was made." -- Marley C.

* * *

"Mistakes are accidents, decisions made quickly -- one did not mean something to happen the way it did. Usually there was not time to put thought into something when a mistake is made. A bad decision is the opposite -- there was time to prepare, to think, weigh all the options. A bad decision is not the end all, another choice just has to be thought of to remedy the effect of the previous decision." -- Vicki H.

* * *

"A mistake is the act of carrying out a bad decision. A bad decision is not a mistake until you act on it. (Goes along with your opening comments about the relation between thought and experience.) -- Gail C.

* * *

"A bad decision is a mistake; recognizing a mistake is how we know it was a bad decision. You got to meet my ex-wife to truly understand." -- Carl E.

* * *

"I think a mistake is a step in the learning process and as such, understandable and worthwhile. A bad decision is a poor choice and one about which you could/should have known better. For example, I made a mistake five years ago when I quit my job, sold my car and moved out to live with some friends in Scottsdale, AZ. It caused me a lot of problems when it did not work out and I was forced to move back to Boston with no job and no money. However, I learned a great deal from this mistake and credit it with many of the correct decisions I have made since.

"An example of a bad decision occurred this past Sunday afternoon. While studying for my Statistics midterm at NYU, I took a break and walked across the street to a campus deli. There are not many people around a campus on a Sunday, particularly during the summer. As a result, the deli keeps a skeleton crew on duty and the food is not fresh. I made a bad decision and ordered chicken with rice. When I brought it back to my study hall, I realized that the chicken was old and inedible. I had to go all the way back there to return it. Choosing the chicken was a bad decision because I should have known better when I thought of the situation." -- Chris W.

* * *

147

What's the difference between a mistake and a bad decision? (continued)

"I like to play word games with this one. I say the word 'mistake' is a shortened version of 'miss take.' A 'take' is anything you 'try to do.' Of course, we only try things expecting we can do them, or that they will turn out successfully. Thereby, a 'miss take' being something that missed the expected target.

"A further thought on 'miss take.' All acts, whether by humans or by nature, have an impact, a result (see 'Chaos Theory'). That result is either intended or unintended. A mistake is an unintended result. And what remains is the new reality . . . to be dealt with, maybe 'corrected' (to get the intended result), or to be lived with.

"Thus endeth the day's lesson." -- Nat E.

* * *

"Mistakes occur out of a sense to 'complete a task QUICKLY,' whereas a bad decision is one made after 'thought has been taken' and an incorrect decision was made." -- Mickey F.

* * *

"You can learn from mistakes but you only beat yourself up for a 'bad' decision. Decisions are turning points or stakes in the ground that start the journey in another direction. If the direction seems less than 'good,' it's time for another decision. Labeling the decision as 'bad' paralyzes the traveler. Sometimes just making any decision is the right thing, because you've continued the journey." -- Joel R.

* * *

"I believe that there are many reasons for making bad decisions -- lack of information, unwillingness to accept realities, pride/stubbornness, arrogance, impatience, unresolved internal conflicts. Such decisions are not inevitable, and can be venal. Mistakes are inevitable. We all make them - it is part of being human, what with all the human frailties - but they are not inherently venal." -- Allan H.

* * *

"Mistake making. This is the easiest one for me. I think the main difference is a mistake is made inadvertently in the course of action, often due to ignorance, inattention or inexperience. A decision, to me, is a conscious process of weighing options and choosing one. Sometimes we make a mistake in this process due to ignorance, inattention, or inexperience, but it may have seemed the best decision at that time. A bad decision is one we make more consciously but go ahead anyway. I hope that makes sense." -- Karin U.

A Lucky Strike?
"If there is such a thing as luck, then I must be the most unlucky fellow in the world. I've never once made a lucky strike in all my life. When I go after something I need, I start finding everything in the world that I don't need -- one damn thing after another. I find 99 things I don't need and then comes number 100 and that -- at the very last -- turns out to be just what I had been looking for."

-- Thomas Edison

Introduction to Goal-Setting

The Perfect Recipe

> *"Aim for the top. There is plenty of room*
> *there. There are so few at the top it*
> *is almost lonely there."*
> *-- Samuel Insull*

Some of life's healthiest recipes aren't found in the cooking section. Instead, they're located under Psychology, in the self-help section, a plethora of books offering a vast array of ingredients to improve your life.

At first glance, these goal-setting recipes appear wholly diverse, each with its own distinctive flair and verve. But beneath the surface I found a striking unity, a common set of ingredients that show up on everyone's "recipe for life."

> *"You have to set new*
> *goals every day."*
> *-- Julie Krone*

Here then are the best of the best -- six ingredients that self-help gurus promise will make your goals irresistibly aromatic.

- ♦ Ingredient #1 -- Write It Down
- ♦ Ingredient #2 -- Think Performance Based
- ♦ Ingredient #3 -- Be Specific
- ♦ Ingredient #4 -- Align Goals With Values
- ♦ Ingredient #5 -- Be Positive
- ♦ Ingredient #6 -- Review, Frequently

Ingredient #1 -- Write 'Em Down

Write 'em down. That's the resolute advice from every self-help chef -- don't just think about your goals, put them on paper. This may appear to be a light-fare recommendation but it's anything but. Chefs insist that the mere act of committing our goals to paper may be the most crucial step in the process. By placing them in print, it immediately fortifies their significance and affirms their existence. Let's be honest -- most of our goals are set privately, and few ever move from mind to matter. The dictate is simple: if you're *truly* interested in achieving your goals, put 'em on paper.

"What three things do you want to accomplish this year? Write them down and place them on your refrigerator for inspiration all year long."

-- source unknown

Ingredient #2 -- Think Performance-Based, Not Outcome-Based

When creating goals, think performance, not outcome. Let's take a classic example -- say you want to lose weight and improve your health. A typical outcome-based goal would be to lose 15 pounds, but the goal is flawed because, technically, it's beyond your control (as are all outcome-based goals).

By contrast, a performance-based goal is within your control. For example, you might decide to work out 30 minutes/day, three times per week, or you might decide to have dessert every other night (instead of every evening). The difference is critical -- performance-based goals are within our control -- action steps that we can *actually take,* while outcome-based goals are beyond our control, often subject to circumstances that we cannot influence (e.g., our body's metabolism).

The message? The more that you focus on your performance, instead of the outcome, the more you'll achieve.

Warning: When Setting Goals, Individual Ingredients May Vary

Cooking Instructions:

Ingredients
- Paper (1)
- Pencil (1)
- Control (1 cup)
- Specificity (1 cup)
- Values (2 cups)
- Positive Attitude (2 tbsp)
- Review (1 tsp)

1. Pre-heat oven to 350 degrees.
2. Pour values into 3 quart bowl.
3. Slowly mix in a positive attitude, control (performance-based) and specificity. Stir thoroughly.
4. Using pencil and paper, write down the appropriate words that describe the goal.
5. Shred paper into bowl, stirring vigorously.
6. Place bowl in oven for 30 minutes, checking frequently to assure that a house fire has not been ignited.
7. Remove from oven.
8. Let goals cool.

Note: If mixture cools too quickly, return to oven and reheat, as desired.

Listen to the folks at Mindtools.com*:

"You should take care to set goals over which you have as much control as possible -- there is nothing as dispiriting as failing to achieve a personal goal for reasons beyond your control such as bad business environments . . . , bad weather, injury, or just plain bad luck. Goals based on outcomes are extremely vulnerable to failure because of things beyond your control.

"If you base your goals on personal performance or skills or knowledge to be acquired, then you can keep control over the achievement of your goals and draw satisfaction from them.

"Review your goals twice every day in order to be focused on achieving them."
-- *Les Brown*

For example, you might achieve a personal best time in a race, but still [fall short of your goal]. If you had set an outcome goal of being in the top three, then this will be a defeat. If you set a performance goal of achieving a particular time, then you will have achieved the goal and can draw satisfaction and self-confidence from its achievement.

"Another flaw is where outcome goals are based on the rewards of achieving something -- whether these are financial or are based on the recognition of colleagues. In early stages these will be highly motivating factors, however as they are achieved, the benefits of further achievement at the same level reduce. You will become progressively less motivated."

"When we are motivated by goals that have deep meaning, by dreams that need completion, by pure love that needs expressing, then we truly live life."

-- Greg Anderson

Jewel Kessler of The Gravity Center defines the difference crisply:

"An outcome goal focuses on an end result. For example, you might have said 'I want to lose 25 pounds.' Or perhaps you mentioned that you want to weigh 125 pounds. . . . A performance goal outlines the process or action taken in an effort to lose weight. A definitive performance goal is 'I will go to my Gravity class and train for 45 minutes,' or 'I will eat five servings of fruits and vegetables each day.'"

Brian Johnston* adds simply:

"Performance goals are associated with less anxiety, since there is flexibility and, as a result, should be emphasized in an exercise and nutrition program. It can be upsetting not to achieve

*Johnston is the Director of Education of the I.A.R.T. Fitness Certification and Education Institute

an outcome goal, but if all the steps leading up to the outcome were done to the best of your ability, it is easy to maintain motivation in preparing for the next outcome goal."

In the athletic arena, performance is what the athlete controls, while "outcomes are frequently controlled by others," explains The Special Olympics, which adds:

"An athlete may have an outstanding performance and not win a contest because other athletes have performed even better. Conversely, an athlete may perform poorly and still win if all other athletes perform at a lower level. If an athlete's goal is to run 12.10 seconds in the 100m, the athlete has greater control in achieving this goal than winning. However, the athlete has even greater control of achieving a goal if the goal is to run using the correct form, driving the knees through the entire race. This performance goal ultimately gives the athlete more control over his/her performance."

"Providence has nothing good or high in store for one who does not resolutely aim at something high or good. A purpose is the eternal condition of success."
-- Thornton T. Munger

They offer two quick examples:

Basketball:
• Outcome: get the rebound
• Performance: make contact with opponent and block out

Football:
• Outcome: get to the ball first, and control it
• Performance: sprint after ball coming into play

Ingredient #3 -- Be Specific

Expert chefs encourage us to create specific, clearly defined goals, to steer clear of generalities. When goals are measurable, definable, precise and quantitative, we stand a greater chance of achieving them. The advice is clear: avoid generalities, disorganization and unsystematic formulation. Be specific.

The experts point the way:

> *"A specific goal has a much greater chance of being accomplished than a general goal. . . . A general goal would be 'Get in shape'. But a specific goal would say, 'Join a health club and workout 3 days a week.'"*
>
> *-- Paul J. Meyer, author of*
> *"Attitude Is Everything"*

"The difference between a goal and a dream is the written word."
-- Gene Donohue

> *"Set specific measurable goals. If you achieve all conditions of a measurable goal, then you can be confident and comfortable in its achievement. If you consistently fail to meet a measurable goal, then you can adjust it or analyze the reason for failure and take appropriate action to improve skills." -- Mind Tools Ltd.**

> *"Consider the difference between these two goals: 1) reduce your unnecessary expenses at home; or 2) reduce personal monthly long distance telephone costs to $45 by July 1, 1995. The second goal sets a specific target for personal phone use. Subconsciously, your mind can now monitor the length of time you spend on long-distance calls." -- Diane M. Eade, Author of "Goal Setting Strategies for a Balanced Life"*

Ingredient #4 -- Align Goals With Values

Experts agree – to achieve your goals, to give them

---

* reproduced with permission, from Mind Tools Ltd., 1996-2012, all rights reserved: http://www.mindtools.com/pages/article/ newHTE_90.htm

What are Your Most Precious Values?

Try this not-so-simple challenge (it'll take you less than two minutes). Grab a pencil, and rank each of the 15 values listed below from 1-10 (an "8" means that the value is of great importance to you, a perfect "10," of course, means it's top shelf). Once you finish the rank order, review how many received a perfect "10" and rank order these. In other words, of the values that you most prize, which of *those* are most important. You might just be surprised at your answer.

___*Comfort*	___*Happiness*	___*Meaningful Job/Career*
___*Contribution/Charity*	___*Health*	___*Recognition*
___*Family*	___*Independence*	___*Religion/Spirituality*
___*Free Time*	___*Long Life*	___*Security*
___*Friendships*	___*Marriage/Signif. Other*	___*Wealth/Money*

a chance to succeed, they must be aligned with your values. There's no other way.

Dr. Scott Mohler, a clinical and organizational psychologist, brilliantly illustrates this point in this classic coaching exchange between business coach (Dr. Mohler) and Michael, a fast-rising manager whose work responsibilities have recently soared.

"If you don't know where you are going, you might wind up someplace else."
-- Yogi Berra

Coach: When we first started meeting, I think you told me that your values include "doing the right thing" and "relentlessly improving." I know there were others you mentioned. I just want to be sure about these two. Have I remembered correctly?

Michael: Yes. That's right.

Coach: Has anything happened since then to change these values?

Michael: No.

Coach: Are you sure? I want to make abso-

lutely certain that these are still your values.

Michael: I'm sure. I believe it's important to act with integrity—do the right thing—and strive to make things better when you can.

Coach: "When you can?" I don't remember that being part of it. "Relentless" means "persistent" or "ceaseless." It doesn't mean when it's easy or convenient or even doable. Again, I want to check with you, is "relentlessly improving" one of your values?

"I feel the most important step in any major accomplishment is setting a specific goal. This enables you to keep your mind focused on your goal and off the many obstacles that will arise when you're striving to do your best."
-- Kurt Thomas

Michael: Yes, sure. That's a very important value of mine. People who know me well would tell you that about me.

Coach: Would you say that you are working to the values of "doing the right thing" and "relentlessly improving" by not addressing the interdivision communication problems we have talked about?

Michael: Probably not. But I'm telling you it won't do any good.

Coach: Well, it depends on what you mean by that. Will pursuing the plan result in improved communications between divisions? Will it translate into better business performance? Will it engage employees by helping them better understand what's going on in their own company? Will you feel like you are leading in a manner consistent with your own values?

Michael: OK. I think I see what you are getting at. I can't get overly focused on the outcome of my actions when the worst that could happen is that they will simply make no difference. I need to pay attention to my values and act accordingly. If I do this, the rest will take care of itself?

Coach: Look, you won't necessarily get the outcome you want all the time. You aren't going to get that no matter what you do. I'm suggesting that you concentrate on the "doing" part and not the final result. I know that runs counter to how many business people think, but this isn't about whether you succeed or fail at some task.

Michael: Are you saying outcomes don't matter?

Coach: I'm not saying that at all. They matter a great deal. But what matters more is how you do what you do. That's what's under your control, and that's what I encourage you to focus on. Let your values set the direction and act in accordance with them. What do your values tell you to do in this situation?

"The goal you set must be challenging. At the same time, it should be realistic and attainable, not impossible to reach It should be challenging enough to make you stretch, but not so far that you break."
-- Rick Hansen

Values, explains Dr. Mohler, stand at the heart of the Value-Based Leadership Coaching (VBLC) method, an empirically grounded counseling approach known as ACT (Acceptance and Commitment Therapy). Dr. Mohler explains that even companies with traditionally rule-bound cultures, such as Walmart, are embracing the management-by-values approach.

And the rules of this game apply equally to individuals -- that is, if you wish to reach your goals, they simply must be in sync with your values.

Ingredient #5 -- Be Positive (Sounds Like A Blood Type)

Be positive, think positive, speak and write in a positive manner. Our chefs concur -- when it comes to the words we speak, the words we think and the words we compose, it's important to "be positive." We must focus on where we are going, not where we have been. This axiom may appear to be a touch of the obvious, but the experts advance this recommendation seriously, citing countless studies about the importance of being positive (as opposed to the importance of being earnest). One need only to turn to the world of sport to gain affirmation to the "positive principle." One memorable study, conducted nearly a decade ago, discovered a single quality that separated the top tennis players in the world from their peers -- their positive "voice." The top athletes used "positive" words to urge themselves on. These players provided concrete evidence that words of encouragement (*"Let's get the next one"*) reign over words that are critical (*"What's wrong with you today?"*).

"What you get by achieving your goals is not as important as what you become by achieving your goals."
-- Zig Ziglar

So no matter your blood type, strive to be positive -- whether you're setting goals or simply talking with yourself. Here's what some pros have to say:

"Write your goal in the positive instead of the negative. Work for what you want, not for what you want to leave behind." -- Gene Donohue of Top Achievement

"Success Questions must be positive. These Success Questions must override your negative internal questions so your subconscious starts working with you instead of against you. . . . Express your goals positively: 'Execute this technique well' is a much better goal than 'don't make this stupid mistake.'"- motivatorpro.com

"Make the goal positive instead of negative. In other words, write what you want to move towards, not what you are trying to move away from. Instead of writing, 'I have lost that unsightly extra 20 pounds,' you could say, 'I weigh a trim, athletic 165 (male or 115 female) pounds.'" -- Anthony Robbins, author of "The Ultimate Success Formula"

(continued on page 160)

Side Dishes

Supplementing our six primary ingredients are a bevy of sauces, condiments and garnishes, each guaranteed to spice up your goals. Here's an assortment to remember.

Remember that goal-setting is a skill -- *"Setting goals at the correct level is a skill that is acquired by practice." -- mindtools.com**

Remember that goals change over time -- *"Remember too that goals change as you mature -- adjust them regularly to reflect this growth in your personality. If goals do not hold any attraction any longer, then let them go. Goal setting is your servant, not your master; it should bring you real pleasure, satisfaction and a sense of achievement." -- mindtools.com**

Remember to set goals when your body is alert -- *"Personal factors such as tiredness, other commitments and the need for rest, etc. should be taken into account when goals are set." -- mindtools.com**

Remember to share your goals cautiously -- *"[U]nless someone is critical to helping you achieve your goal(s), keep your goals to yourself. The negative attitude from friends, family and neighbors can drag you down quickly. It's very important that your self-talk (the thoughts in your head) are positive." -- Gene Donohue of Top Achievement*

Remember to enjoy your successes, and enjoy the process --*"Make a concerted effort to enjoy each milestone as you travel the road to success; don't waste time worrying about goals you haven't yet reached. Keep your expectations realistic: No one reaches all of his or her goals. Remember that progress is always ongoing. Relax, and enjoy the process." -- Diane M. Eade, author of "Goal-Setting: Strategies for a Balanced Life"*

* reproduced with permission, from Mind Tools Ltd., 1996-2012, all rights reserved: http://www.mindtools.com/pages/article/newHTE_90.htm

Ingredient #6 -- Review, Frequently

It's important to recall that when you take your main dish out of the oven (think: turkey, Thanksgiving) you still must tend to its needs: Is it cooked thoroughly? How long must it cool? Is it ready to slice? Will it need extra sauce?

As so it is with goals. Once set, once out of the oven, we must tend to its needs, constantly reviewing and revising. The world's goal-setting gurus offer a panoply of recommendations on how often we should revisit our goals, but the consensus is clear: the more the better -- once a week for certain, but once a day is not too often. The point is, the more that you're thinking about your goals, the more opportunity you'll have to shape in ways that you desire. The experts weigh in:

> *"Have a set of goals for every day and review the results every night. It may seem like a lot of time and trouble, but isn't making a success of your life worth it? It's not the trouble that bothers you, it's the discipline. Think that through, because if you're not willing to accept your own discipline, you're not going to accomplish 2% of what you could and you'll miss out on 98% of the good things you could have. . . . Just think about it. Most people spend more time planning for a vacation than they do planning for their lives."*
> *-- Tom Hopkins, author of "How to Master the Art of Selling"*

Making Time
"You will never find time for anything. If you want time, you must make it."
> *-- Charles Bixton*

Rule #18
Zero to One

"The secret of getting ahead
is getting started."
-- Sally Berger

Think of yourself as a master chef, wielding a sharply honed carving knife, capable of slicing goals into bite-sized pieces. This is the message of Rule 18 -- think small, think bite-sized, think zero to one (not zero to ten).

Rule 18 is the salve for our human tendency to over-commit and over-promise -- not just to others but to ourselves. Rarely a day goes by when we don't make a private promise that, however well intentioned, commits us to too vast a course of action. Still, we continue to over indulge, intent on going back for seconds (zero to ten) when we know that a single portion will do (zero to one).

"Setting goals for your game is an art. The trick is in setting them at the right level, neither too low nor too high."
-- Greg Norman

The solution? Zero to one. Whether you're planning to spend more time with your children, explore a career change, reduce your monthly expenses, initiate an exercise program, study for a major exam or launch a new business, it's critical to keep the carving knife close at hand. After all, a thick piece of bread is far more likely to get stuck in your throat than a dollop.

Often, in setting personal goals, we trap ourselves by using code words like "every" and "never" ("I'm going to work out every day," or "I'm never going to order cake for dessert"). Our irrepressible urge to leap from "zero to ten" touches every part of our lives. It affects:

♦ Our relationships, when we move too quickly;

♦ Our financial lives, when we buy items we can't afford;

♦ Our work lives, when we assume too many tasks, in an unbounded bid to both please and impress.

The Answer?

Zero to one. When we slice our goals into bite-sized pieces we overcome one of life's supreme hurdles -- getting started. Our first step is always the hardest -- whether we're searching for a new job or a new mate, finishing a term paper or a business plan. The most difficult step is always the first; once taken, a body in motion *does* tend to stay in motion.

"A good beginning makes a good end."
-- English Proverb

Thinking small helps us begin (see my friend's wonderful story, on the next page). Thinking "zero to one" helps us set goals that are realistic and attainable. And it paves the way for setting follow-on goals, from two to three, then three to four. When we set goals incrementally, we leave ourselves room to grow *and* room to slide. If we're sitting at level five and somehow fail, we have plenty of room to backslide . . . to level four, or level three.

But when we start with zero to ten (*"I'm going to start walking a mile every day"*), and then fail, we tend to slide back . . . to zero.

Shock of Shocks: The Goal Slicer Works!

To my friends, I offered the following challenge: select a personal goal (I asked them to choose a simple one), then try to cut it in half, then half again. The idea was to find out if cutting a goal in half (or half again) made it more palatable, more do-able.

Here's what my close friend Nat Emery had to say:

"Goal: Clean my house by Thursday. (Thursday is critical because I have a walk through by a potential buyer . . . boy, if that doesn't generate some questions, you're losing your edge!)

"1st Slice: Clean half my house by Thursday. (Notice I didn't slice it the other way . . . Clean my house by Tuesday!) OK. That's probably more realistic, anyway.

"2nd Slice: Clean only the first floor. But you can't do just that. The walk through, remember?

"3rd Slice: Clean only the Living Room. Wait a minute! You can do more than that! (The voices of criticism and social awareness are very loud!)

"I cannot do less! Doing less than the whole house is looming larger and more urgent than before I started the exercise! What is causing that? I WILL do the entire house. In fact, I have just made two phone calls to solicit extra help! So what did the slicing do? I'm not sure. In this case it deepened the resolve. Will it always? I suspect it might! A new twist to setting goals . . . and actually meeting them!

"Thanks, Steve!"

Think about it. Think about the last time you set a goal and, after failing to achieve it, ended up doing nothing.

That's what makes zero to ten so impossible, it leaves little room for retreat, little margin for error.

You know the feeling. It's that moment when you're about to start the bills, clean the yard, prepare a report, start the laundry, practice the piano or place pictures in the family album. Inevitably, the hardest part is "getting started." That's what makes Rule 18 so vital.

Just Begin

In its simplest form, Rule 18 boils down to a single word: begin. When a task stands before us, our greatest challenge is simply to start, to commence, to engage. Our tendency, of course, is to stare at the mountaintop, overwhelmed by its size and its slope. But if we are to make the ascent, if we are to reach the crest, we must find a way to *start* instead of *stare*.

"Though no one can go back and make a brand new start, anyone can start from now and make a brand new ending."

-- Carl Bard

These are the moments to unsheath our knife and start slicing, these are the moments to identify "rest stops" on the trail, to make our ascent more palatable.

Why is "zero to one" so difficult? Because of our ego, that ever-sensitive part of our psyche that jumps at the slightest provocation. Here's a typical scenario:

You've just set a goal to walk 30 minutes a day, five days a week (I'd label this a "zero to ten" goal). Days later, after you realize you've over-commited, you decide to dramatically revise your plan and begin, instead, with "zero to one." Translation: you decide to start with three minutes a day, three days a week.

"Three minutes! What, are you kidding?"

Your ego has arrived, that ever-familiar self-critical internal voice that begs for attention.

"Three minutes is ridiculous. What good will that do? What difference will that make?"

It's time to tell your captious ego to back off, to relax,

to just listen. It's time to explain that three minutes a day achieves two fundamental aims:

1. It moves you off of zero; and
2. It creates a new pattern of behavior.

Three minutes *does* make a difference, not just by creating a new modus operandi but by bolstering you physically and mentally. Your ego will be slow to agree (remember, it's not exactly a world-class listener), but if it can hear you at all, remind it that success breeds success and that by thinking small, thinking do-able, you're moving forward.

Some years ago I created a "zero to one" goal that began with a single pushup. Sure, I laughed, because a single pushup seemed absurd. And again, on day two, when I added a second, I laughed again; after all, my entire workout had just lasted for four seconds. But as the days pressed on, there I was, doing nine pushups on day nine and 21 on day 21. What started as a comically small exercise had become, in just three weeks, a major personal triumph.

"If you want to get there, begin; it's a rule so unusually simple that most people have immense difficulty learning it."
-- Hugh Prather

Please, No Laughing

So the next time you approach a task of drudgery, think zero to one. First identify the challenge, then start trimming, in a bid to make a mountain look more like a mole hill. No judgment. No admonition. And please, no laughter.

Instead, be kind to yourself (Rule #1) and climb at a comfortable pace. Take the next step when you're ready. Others will push you to race up the stairs -- and many will chide you for not climbing faster. Ignore them. Resist temptation.

Think bite-sized. Think small. Think zero to one.

Challenge 18A
How Sharp Is Your Knife?

When the moment is right, try this Thought Experiment.

Step 1: Select a personal goal. There's no need to write it down, just select it mentally. If a specific goal doesn't come to mind, feel free to create one. The size of the goal is irrelevant.

Step 2: Mentally slice the goal in half.* Example: you plan to clean out the garage, so you slice the goal in half, and decide to clean just one section.

Step 3: Slice in half again . . . then again. Continue slicing your goal in half *until you begin to hear the harsh voice of self-criticism,* that is, when your inside voice cries out: "You can do more than that, you can do better!" That's when you know that you've sliced it enough to get started.

Example #1
Goal: to practice the piano for 40 minutes a day.
Slice #1: 20 minutes ("*20 minutes, yes, I can do that*");
Slice #2: 10 minutes (*"That's not very much"*);
Slice #3: 5 minutes (*"Five minutes? Are you kidding?"*).

Example #2
Goal: to walk two miles every day (*"I can do that; that's only a half hour a day; I'll do it right after work; maybe Roe will join me"*);
Slice #1: one mile a day (*"OK, maybe two miles is too much; I'll do a mile a day; yes, that's a good start"*).
Slice #2: a half mile
Slice #3: a quarter mile, or four minutes/day (*"Oh come on, just four minutes? You must be kidding! You can spare more than that!"*)
Steeled to continue, I slice again.
Slice #4: an eighth of a mile, or two minutes/day (*"Are you serious? It takes more than 2 minutes to tie your sneakers. That's ridiculous, you slacker."*)

OK, OK, I yield to the internal voices of criticism.

---

* *Note: many goals don't lend themselves to slicing, so please select one that does. For example: a goal to "become a better friend" might be difficult (though not impossible), to slice in half, while a goal to learn a new recipe each month might not.*

The Author's Friends Share Their Thoughts
In a bid to learn how others think, the author assembled a panel of 30 friends (psychologists and social workers among them) to answer some of life's most penetrating questions. Excerpts of their answers appear below.

The author asked his friends:
When slicing goals in half, when does your PGA (personal goal analyzer) become self-critical?

"My PGA reaches the critical point the more I slice my goal. Although, I must admit I feel the internal process of analyzing the goal and my actions toward achieving the goal immediately (it must be my sales orientation which is results driven).

"Case and point was exercising this week. I just had to do it despite all the rationalization of other "priorities" that are on that unending list. Once you make the decision to move forward toward achieving your goal there is strong personal satisfaction. There is no question that establishing aggressive goals can be self-defeating. Developing a plan to achieve that goal needs to be part of the process. I recently read a speech from the CEO of Coke. He stated 'yesterday is history, tomorrow is a mystery, the present is a gift.' I like to treat all my goals as immediately achievable. Unfortunately, this is unrealistic. However, as long as there is a plan and it is in motion, I can feel gratification.

"Now, time for vacation. My goal is to relax and enjoy." -- Sheila F.

*   *   *

Author: Does your PGA reach critical mass at any point, or does it gradually move to self-criticism? In other words, is it typically two slices and out, or are there cases where your PGA can handle four slices, or even five?

"As far as my PGA reaching a critical point . . . I am inclined to say that it would, that it is 2-3 slices for self criticism to peak. I will try to be more cognizant in this area and bring my findings to our 'dinner session'."-- Sheila F.

*   *   *

"I get disgusted more often by breaking patterns that I consider important than I do by my lack of initiative to start new ones. Step 1 is important but approach/avoidance for me usually comes in the form a piece of cake when I am on a diet. And sooner or later, I am going to eat that piece of cake. So why go on the diet, at least until I feel that I have the fortitude to offend a nice little old lady with a dish of cookies in her hand . . . I don't think this answers the question, but it's where I am." -- Carl E.

Watch Your Beginnings
"Let us watch well our beginnings, and results will manage themselves."

-- Alexander Clark

Toughest Distance to Cover
A journalist once posed this question to an 85 year old marathoner who had run races around the world: "What's the toughest distance to cover?"

Anticipating that the runner might mention the Himalayas, or the plains of Africa, he instead paused and answered:

"The toughest distance to cover . . . is the eight feet from my bed to my sneakers, on a cold wintry January morning, before the sun rises. If you can cover that distance, you can do anything."

Rule #19
Be Firm, Yet Flexible

"In between goals is a thing called life,
that has to be lived and enjoyed."
                              -- Sid Caesar

How flexible are you?

I don't mean in the physical sense, though I envy people who have supple limbs (like my wife, fast becoming a yoga expert). Instead, I'm talking about mental flexibility, that elusive yet subtle quality that enhances our lives, in a million little ways.

For years, I equated flexibility with weakness, with vulnerability and lack of conviction (I'm a male, so you understand). I prided myself on standing firm, no matter the forum. How misguided.

"Life is a rollercoaster.
Try to eat a light lunch."
-- David A. Schmaltz

Today, I view firm and flex as equals -- "firm" is the motivating force which helps us reach our goals, while "flex" is the moderating force which helps us balance life priorities.

Whether we're trying to learn a new recipe, to stop smoking, to leave the office by 5, to spend more time with the grandchildren, to switch jobs, to start a workout program, or to sign up for dance lessons, the Firm-Flex Continuum (FFC) is always in play, a hidden traveler on every excursion.

The Firm-Flex Continuum

Flexible 0.10.20.30.40.50.60.70.80.90.100 **Firm**

The message is simple: we must constantly balance our desire to be firm (i.e., to pursue our goal) with our need to be flexible (i.e., to relax our pursuit when higher priorities intervene).

And though the Firm-Flex Continuum applies to the full sweep of human interactions, from relationships (*"I should have been a little more flexible in my approach"*) to commitments (*"I should have been a touch more firm in saying no"*), its greatest service is in helping us reach our goals.

"It is inevitable that some defeat will enter even the most victorious life. The human spirit is never finished when it is defeated . . . it is finished when it surrenders."

-- Ben Stein

The Firm-Flex Continuum comes into play *after* we've set our goal, after we've declared our intention to our friends, our spouse or our co-workers. The Firm-Flex Continuum helps us address the hardest part of the goal-setting process -- *the follow-through.* Let's be honest, as difficult as it may be to *set* goals, the true test comes after we've set them. This is where Rule 19 shines.

Example #1: A Health Club Debut

Rule 19 was unveiled in the most unlikely of places -- a neighborhood health club, on a Concept I rowing machine. I was sitting next to a woman (also rowing), when we began to talk about exercise and commitment. Soon enough, I posed this scenario:

Let's say that you begin an exercise program with the hope of walking 20 minutes a day, three days a week. The moment you voice your decision, your commitment is firm -- you're probably up near 90 on the Firm-Flex Continuum (0 = total flex, 100 = total firm).

Two weeks later, as you evaluate your progress, you rate yourself an "85." You think to yourself: "it's been a great couple of weeks."

But suddenly, faster than you can say "speed bump," the tide turns -- your boss asks you to take over a troubled project, the dog gets deathly ill and your friend needs support as her relationship nears the breaking point. All too quickly, time becomes your most precious resource. It's now impossible *just to do what you have to do.*

What now?

Time to flex, time to slide down the scale and say to yourself: "Hey, I've been really firm about this; perhaps it's time to be a touch more flexible." You decide to slide down to "30", commiting to walk twice a week, 10 minutes each time.

> *"You don't drown by falling in the water; you drown by staying there."*
> *-- Edwin Louis Cole*

The key? YOU'RE STILL WALKING. You didn't quit. And as circumstances change, as you know they will, you'll retain the option to charge back up the scale, back toward firm.

Firm to flex, flex to firm, and back again. This is the glory of the FFC, allowing us the mental freedom to relax our deadlines *without having to fully surrender.*

Example #2: Vacation Time

You're suffering under the dictate of a new diet, struggling to push yourself past week #2. The truth is, you've been quite firm, diligently cataloguing your food intake, passing up seconds more than you care to remember. If you had to guess, you'd rank yourself an "80." But now, a day before your vacation, you're worried that your diet is in jeopardy.

What now?

Think flex. Remind yourself that a slide down to "30" or "20" is quite appropriate for vacation. Once back in the nest, you'll have time to firm it up. The key is: *you're still on the diet;* you're just being flexible.

Example #3: The Bedroom

"Saturday. This Saturday." You say the words out loud: "I'm going to finish painting that bedroom this Saturday." You've spent weeks gathering materials and prepping the walls, so you're primed. And Saturday appears a lock until, suddenly, you learn that your brother-in-law needs post-surgery support this weekend.

"Notice the difference between what happens when a man says to himself, I have failed three times, and what happens when he says, I am a failure."

-- S.I. Hayakawa

Think flex.

Firm to flex, flex to firm, and back again. The trick is to never leave the continuum, to never abandon ship. Go ahead and relocate your tent, just don't pack it up and take it home. Too often, when our resolve wanes, we ride the wave to "0," never pausing long enough to check the view from "30", "20" or "10."

What's wrong with stopping at "30?" What's wrong with employing a touch of flexibility?

The Supreme Motivator

In its brightest light, the FFC is The Supreme Motivator, helping us stay fixed on our goals. And in its passionate moments, Firm-Flex is The Ultimate Salve, helping us temper frustration, without surrender.

Not long after I shared the notion of Firm-Flex with my rowing mate I began to realize that every notion, every intention, every goal, possessed its own Firm-Flex Continuum. My desire to create a flower garden, finish the holiday shopping, build a new cabinet, prepare a newly revised family budget -- each contained elements

---

Challenge 19A
While Lying in Bed ...

Tomorrow morning, when you're lying in bed, call to mind a personal goal and ask yourself this simple question:

> *"On the Firm-Flex Continuum,*
> *where do I sit today?"*

Once you fix your spot, ask yourself the following:

> *"In which direction do I wish to head today*
> *-- toward firm or toward flex?"*

You just might be surprised at your answer.

---

of firm and flex. The challenge, of course, is to find that comfortable balance. So, increasingly, I began to pose two questions:

1. On the Firm-Flex Continuum, where do I sit today? and, equally important,

2. Today, in which direction do I wish to head?"

The questions were liberating because they allowed me the freedom to move forward, and the freedom to let go. In writing this book, I probably used Rule 19 more than any single rule. Time and again I would set "firm" deadlines, only to find that life -- in its inimitable way -- would get in the way. As my frustration rose, over a missed deadline, or a chapter that demanded more research, I tried to "flex," to ease off a bit and simply relax. Not that Rule 19 dissolved all my worries. It didn't. But it did help remind me that, when pursuing goals of substance, a dose of flexibility goes a long way.

Rule 19's message is simple: allow yourself to ride

"We come into this world head first and go out feet first; in between, it is all a matter of balance."

-- Paul Boese

173

freely on the Firm-Flex Continuum, and switch directions, as needed.

When Your Will Wanes

"One of the secrets of life is to make stepping stones out of stumbling blocks."

-- Jack Penn

The reality is, days or weeks or months after you've set your goal, your resolve will weaken. This is the moment for which Rule 19 was built -- the "waning moment." When your determination declines, when your will wanes, Rule 19 will help you persevere, help you stay engaged.

So when your will wanes, craft a new script. Don't surrender, or resign, or quit, just flex. And remind yourself that they'll be plenty of opportunities to slide back toward "firm," when the moment is right.

Firm to flex, flex to firm, and back again.

Bouncing Back
"I don't measure a man's success by how high he climbs but how high he bounces when he hits bottom." -- George S. Patton

Quitting Too Soon
"Many men fail because they quit too soon. They lose faith when the signs are against them. They do not have the courage to hold on, to keep fighting in spite of that which seems insurmountable. If more of us would strike out and attempt the 'impossible', we very soon would find the truth of that old saying that nothing is impossible . . . " -- Dr. C.E. Welch

More on firm-flex:
- ♦ *Appendix J: "How Many Bumps Have You Had Today?" (p211)*
- ♦ *Appendix K: "Are You a Light Switch or a Dimmer?" (p213)*

Challenge 19B
"Out to Lunch, Be Back in an Hour"

Too often, when our goals go awry, we abandon them altogether. We start a new diet, stay on it for weeks, then drop it like a hot potato (which, by the way, isn't on the diet at all).

Why do we react so hastily? Why do we decide to take a permanent vacation when we simply could have placed a sign in the window that read: "Out to Lunch, Be Back in an Hour"?

This is the lifeblood of Rule 19: taking a simple break -- a break from goal pursuit -- without waiving the white flag. Let's take a look at a typical goal-setting cycle, to learn how we might use Firm-Flex.

Stage 1: From Desire to Goal

A goal begins with a notion, a thought, a whim. We mentally contemplate a desire -- i.e., to travel to Europe, to improve our dancing skills, to pursue a new job -- then begin the process of floating the idea to various parts of our subconscious. The strongest desires take root and soon our mind's eye creates an informal goal statement. If the desire strengthens we begin more concrete activities -- we share the goal with a friend (verbal commitment) or jot it down (written commitment). Excitement starts to build.

Stage 2: Goal Pursuit, The Early Days

The first days go exceptionally well -- your commitment has taken on a life of its own and you're thrilled at your level of energy. On the Firm-Flex Continuum, you're sitting pretty at "90."

Stage 3: Caution: Speed Bumps

Down the road -- be it days, weeks or months -- the bumps begin to appear, perhaps from work, a family illness, unanticipated bills or times of conflict with a family member. Make no mistake, the bumps *will* arrive. And each bump, in its own way, will impede your ability to reach your personal goal.

Stage 4: Bump Control (Enter Firm-Flex)

This is the critical stage in goal pursuit, the stage where 95%

of our goals are abandoned. How best to navigate the "bumps?" By reminding yourself that bumps are inevitable and that you, and you alone, can delay your goals without abandoning them. In short, it's time to flex. Instead of waiving the white flag (or throwing in the towel), just flex.

Stage 5: Firm to Flex, Flex to Firm, and Back Again

If you've reached Stage 5, let me first offer my congratulations -- you've obviously passed the GPB (the Great Psychological Barrier). Reaching Stage 5 means that you've embraced reality, that you refuse to let some minor interference jeopardize your goals. You set your diet, and you've been good, really good. But the holidays are here and relatives are visiting, and the food on your neighbor's coffee table tastes too good to abstain. You enjoy. But in so doing you remind yourself that, today, you're simply being flexible, and that tomorrow, as the day unfolds, you might decide to travel toward North, toward firm. Firm to flex, flex to firm, and back again.

A Mental Pit Stop

The beauty of Rule 19 is that it creates a mental pit-stop -- a time out, a pause, from the relentless demands of goal pursuit. Instead of yielding to the internal voice that surrenders . . .

> *"It's too hard."*
> *"I don't have time."*
> *"This is just too much trouble."*

You have a choice. You can hang out a sign that reads:

Store Closed – Liquidation Sale

or one that says:

Out to Lunch – Be Back in an Hour

Save some fries for me.

Rule #20

Set Goals,
Not Expectations
Not the product

"Expect nothing, live frugally on surprise."
                              -- Alice Walker

Where do our expectations come from?

It's not as if we wake up in the morning and ask ourselves, "Hmmm, what expectations should I have today?" Imagine sitting at the kitchen table, pen and pad in hand, and jotting down a list of expectations for the year ahead. Sounds crazy, no?

Goals, of course, are different -- we consciously set them. We set them privately, with our thoughts, and publicly, with our tongues. Every time we create a personal goal -- to build a colorful garden, lower our handicap, redecorate, lose weight or sign up for tennis lessons -- we do so consciously, with forethought and intention.

"I can teach anybody how to get what they want out of life. The problem is that I can't find anybody who can tell me what they want."
                              -- Mark Twain

Not so with expectations. Expectations simply appear, no forethought, no planning. Think about it: when was the last time that you attended a seminar on "Setting Expectations?" I'm sure that it's been a while, making it ever more questionable why we allow expectations to steer our ship. Why is that?

177

Expectations are the *natural byproduct* of the goal-setting process, or so it seems. Our conscious mind sets a goal and BOOM!, our subconscious immediately creates a parallel, matching expectation. I suppose one could argue that expectations are a motivating force, that having aggressive expectations help us reach our goal.

I beg to differ. I believe that expectations are the scourge of our psychological existence, that they interfere with our climb, that they discourage and deflate us, raising false hopes and painting unflattering pictures.

Let's be done with them.

"Decide what you want, decide what you are willing to exchange for it. Establish your priorities and go to work."

-- H.L. Hunt

Expectations are like unwanted guests -- they arrive at your party, uninvited and unannounced. They consume vast quantities of food and stay for unreasonable lengths of time. And, when you ask them to leave, in a cordial and congenial tone, they simply refuse.

Expectations are the invisible -- some would say insidious -- part of the goal-setting process. We don't consciously create them, yet their inevitable presence shapes our experience and dominates our thoughts. Is it possible to create goals without expectations?

Try this 60-second thought experiment. Place the book aside for a moment and create a personal goal -- something small, something modest. After the goal is set, pause for 15 seconds and ask yourself whether your mind has, unconsciously, created a parallel expectation. Go ahead, we'll wait.

Our Constant Companions

Like it or not, expectations are our constant companions, partners in every goal and every endeavor. They give voice to our hopes (*"My game will be stronger*

Setting Goals for Our Friends?

It's a crazy notion. But consider this: is it possible to have goals without expectations?

Or expectations without goals?

When we deal with ourselves, we usually have both -- we set a goal, and then, in a flash, an expectation comes to life. But when we deal with our friends, there are *only expectations*, no goals to consider (though consider, for a moment, how different life would be if we set goals for our friends).

Which leads to our fundamental question: if it's possible to have expectations without goals (as with our friends), is it possible to have goals without expectations?

---

after I take some lessons") and voice to our fears *("I don't expect to get the job"*).

Whether we're engaged in a serious relationship, sipping a cup of hot tea, hopping a cab to the airport or taking our child's temperature to check for fever, expectations envelope our thoughts: I *expect* my friend to be more supportive, I *expect* the chamomile tea to have a sweeter taste, I *expect* light traffic on the way to the airport, I *expect* the thermometer to be working.

"I'm not in this world to live up to your expectations and you're not in this world to live up to mine."
-- Frederick Perls

At times our expectations are easily known and freely articulated. But often we're unaware that they exist. Often it's not until the moment has passed that we realize our *expectation* was the cause of our irritation. Few would dispute that our lives would be happier if we could cast aside our expectations. Where better to start than with our goals?

Whether our goal is to nab the next contract, spend more time with our children, or finish cleaning the kitchen by 7 o'clock, our expectations -- not our goals -- shape our thoughts, our state of mind. *It doesn't have to be that way.* Instead, let's build a mental viewfinder that ignores expectations, that sees only goals . . . and the steps needed to reach them.

Expectations serve no purpose. they simply delay and distract us, and inhibit our ability to meet our goals. So be gone with them. Let's use our private time to prepare for the challenges ahead.

Purge, Baby, Purge

"You are a product of your environment. So choose the environment that will best develop you toward your objective. Analyze your life in terms of its environment. Are the things around you helping you toward success -- or are they holding you back?"
-- W. Clement Stone

Rule 20's missive is simple: eradicate your expectations and free yourself. How best to shed? Try these simple tips:

Tip #1. Acknowledge (Open Your Eyes)

Acknowledge the reality -- that goals and expectations typically are co-dependent, that it's nearly impossible to have a personal goal without an accompanying expectation. Don't waste your time trying to convince yourself that you don't have expectations (about where the relationship is going, about whether you'll receive the promotion). Just acknowledge that the expectation is there.

Tip #2. Understand (Open Your Ears)

Examine your expectations, take time to learn about them. Soon after you set a goal ask yourself these simple questions: What do I expect will happen? What am I basing my expectation on? Is it realistic or not? To what degree has my expectation been influenced by relatives, friends and associates?

Where Do Our Expectations Come From?

From our family?
Our friends?
Our teachers?
Our neighbors?
TV scriptwriters?
Playwrights and pundits?

One can safely assume that expectations evolve from a blend of our experiences -- what we see, and hear, and perceive -- and our brain's chemistry, that is, the neural connections that make us who we are.

The process might be as simple as: 1. we perceive an external event; 2. our brain interprets it; and 3. our brain stores this information for "recall" when forming judgments or making decisions. The question I bid you explore is: "In the world of expectations, to what degree are we influenced by our environment, by the opinions and attitudes of those with whom we interact?"

Tip #3. Jettison (Put Those Arms in Motion)

Purge, baby, purge. It's time to purge your system of those crippling expectations. But be patient, because change takes time (ah, Rule 20 even works on itself -- it's best not to have expectations about eliminating them). But change is possible, if only we take the time to become more aware of what goes on inside our head.

"Our desires always disappoint us; for though we meet with something that gives us satisfaction, yet it never thoroughly answers our expectation."
-- Francois De La Rochefoucauld

In truth, our challenge isn't so much to *eliminate* our expectations as to move past them, to re-channel our energy into action steps to reach our goal. Let's be honest . . .

. . . expectations don't help us sharply

define our goals -- our ability to focus does that;

. . . expectations don't help us pursue our goals -- our ability to persist does that; and

. . . expectations don't help us adjust in mid-stream -- our flexibility does that.

So set goals . . . not expectations.

More on expectations vs. goals:

Appendix L:
"We Have Very High Expectations
of our Students"
(p215)

Rule #21

Question All Rules

"If you obey all the rules,
you miss all the fun."
-- Katherine Hepburn

When I asked my daughter Melyssa if she remembers Rule 21, she usually smiles and says: "Sure, I remember Rule 21. Isn't that 'Break all Rules?' " She was 19 at the time, so you understand.

Though Melyssa was being playful, akin to the rule itself, she and her sisters rarely miss an opportunity to dust off Rule 21 and take it out for a spin. Naturally we, the parents, are the spin-ees.

Rules are a natural battleground between parent and child because they pit the parent's basic instinct to protect (*"In bed by 9"*) against the child's natural desire to rebel (*"Just one more show?"*). But Rule 21 applies to far more than parenting and teenage rebellion; it touches every corner of our lives.

"There are no exceptions to the rule that everybody likes to be an exception to the rule."
-- Charles Osgood

We have rules for romance and rules of the sea, we have house rules and zoning rules, rules of etiquette and rules of the road -- not to mention game rules (plenty of those!) and golden rules. Rules follow us to the kitchen (*"no snacks before dinner time"*), not to mention the classroom (*raise your hand before speaking**).

Let's face it. Human beings are incessant rulemakers, creating rules to order our lives and inject a measure of stability in an overly complex world. No institution does this better than the federal government, which each year drafts thousands of rules to codify our laws (years ago, the IRS alone had more than 700 tax rules under development). But rulemaking isn't just the province of lawmakers. Individuals, families, corporations and religious groups craft a thousand little rules to guide our every step, our every action.

"Absolutely speaking, Do unto others as you would that they should do unto you is by no means a golden rule, but the best of current silver. An honest man would have but little occasion for it. It is golden not to have any rule at all in such a case."
-- Henry David Thoreau

Q: "Why can't I return this for a cash refund?"
A: "I'm sorry, Madam, that's just our policy."

Forgive me, but I need to know *why* -- why is this policy still in place? Does it still apply? Does it still make sense?

Challenge Early, Challenge Often

Rule 21 encourages us to challenge *every* rule, both those we create and those we encounter. Our final rule turns an age-old adage: "*Rules are made to be broken,*" into a one-word maxim:

"Challenge."

Rule 21 urges us to both ask the question *and* listen patiently to the answer. By doing so, we'll be in better

* My friend and educator Marley Casagrande shares these insightful words about class rules: "When teachers talk about class 'rules,' I prefer to call them 'circumstances that are necessary for everyone to learn and be safe,' which seems more positive and conducive to building a learning community. For example, instead of having a rule, 'Don't interrupt while someone is talking,' I like, 'Show respect by listening to others as they are talking, and expect them to do the same.'"

position to challenge the rule. But unless we ask why, we risk letting impulsivity, not intellect, guide our actions.

Rules Beyond Reason

Few institutions, including families, can say that they house no antiquated rules. Every community -- that is, every community of human beings -- owns rules beyond reason. For example:

• Girls aren't supposed to call boys for dates;
• The doctor doesn't adjust the bill if you're waiting for an hour;
• The catalog company won't consider an ordered item "lost" until six weeks have passed;
• You're required to wear a collared shirt on most golf courses, but the quality of the shirt doesn't matter, it simply has to have a collar.

"No statement should be believed because it is made by an authority."
-- Hans Reichenbach

Rules beyond reason? My good friend Vicki Sullivan shares one of her favorites:

"My favorite sermon was delivered by one of the priests at St. John Neumann on this very subject: rules of religion that are blindly obeyed, die hard but, once they do, you question why they were ever important. He cited several examples, but my favorite, by far, was the rule that a woman's head must be covered before entering the church. This was abolished (or whatever they do to cancel religious rules) many years ago, but he remembers women going to great lengths to cover their heads with any available tissue, scarf, handkerchief, etc. if they had forgotten their little lace pocket mantilla (or doily, as we fondly called it). He said he had seen it all, but the woman that won the award for ingenuity in a desperate moment was the woman who dashed into mass at the last moment wearing an empty pack of Marlboro's bobby-pinned to the top of

her head."

The problem, it seems, is not that we have antiquated rules, but that we so often fail to test them.

Parental Survival Tips

Typical of all parents, Roe and I were often challenged on house rules (e.g., curfews, driving restrictions) and our parental survival was linked to two words -- health and safety. When our teenage crew asked *"Why?"* we answered: *"Health and Safety."*

"Nothing strengthens authority so much as silence."
-- Charles De Gaulle

For the most part, the answer seemed to satisfy because our daughters came to understand the reasons underpinning our house rules and the values that they promote. Not that they willingly agreed -- they often didn't -- but they did embrace the logic and, at some level, found it comforting to know that we care. Periodically, of course, the message was lost in a series of verbal battles linked to power and control. But when a parent sets an evening curfew, they're promoting safety. And when they urge "lights out," they're promoting health. And so with a million minor urgings in the words between parent and child.

To be certain, parents set rules that go beyond health and safety -- e.g., *"no playtime before chores are finished,"* or *"homework finished before dinner"* -- and these bear right to legitimate challenge. So too in the marketplace, where countless policies -- e.g., *no carryover of vacation time* -- stand ready for challenge. This is the province of Rule 21.

Playing By the Rules

So, the next time that you're told to play by the rules, ask for a copy of them. And the next time that you realize that your *own* rule is flawed, go ahead and change it, even if you created it a moment ago.

But remember. When you decide to challenge a rule, keep Rule 12 (Be Kind, To Others) close at hand, because a hostile challenge inevitably leads to a hostile response.

So challenge early, and often. But do so with compassion and grace.

You'll live longer.

Do the Wrong Thing

"When great operas do touch directly on the problem of how to live, the advice they give is rarely didactic and never obvious. Take, for example, Mozart's Cosi Fan Tutte and Britten's Billy Budd. On the surface, these two operas would seem to have little in common. One is a quicksilver comedy of manners, the other a pitch-black tragedy constructed on a grand scale. But both have a 'moral' -- though not the kind you're likely to find in Aesop -- and what's more, the morals are identical: if you want to lead a happy life, be prepared to break a few rules."

-- advice from Terry Teachout, writer for Opera News, in a piece he crafted titled "Do the Wrong Thing."

The Author's Friends Share Their Thoughts
In a bid to learn how others think, the author assembled a panel of 30 friends (psychologists and social workers among them) to answer some of life's most penetrating questions. Excerpts of their answers appear below.

The author asked his friends:
What rules make no sense?

[Author's Note: In addition to the above query, I asked my friends to offer their own "golden rule." Here's what they had to say.]

"Rules that don't make sense: Girls aren't supposed to call boys for dates." -- Ilene F.

* * *

"The Golden Rule: Whoever has the Gold Rules. Think about it . . . then smile . . . then think about it. . . ." -- Jerry S.

* * *

"I have some strong feelings about rules. I don't like the word in some cases, although I know rules are necessary and welcome in many situations. However, rules may need to be broken, and consideration should be given to those situations in which not breaking the rule may have more severe consequences than breaking it, although I realize it depends on how you look at things!

"The Constitution contains some of the most important rules of all, but they're not called RULES! In Fairfax County Schools, we have a handbook of Student Responsibilities and Rights. I like the word 'responsibility' far better than 'rule' when it comes to discipline, since 'rule' implies blind compliance rather than the conscious assumption of responsibility.

"When teachers talk about class 'rules', I prefer to call them 'circumstances that are necessary for everyone to learn and be safe', which seems more positive and conducive to building a learning community. For example, instead of having a rule, 'Don't interrupt while someone is talking', I like, 'Show respect by listening to others as they are talking, and expect them to do the same'. If we understand WHY this rule, or expectation, is in place, we are more likely to 'follow the rule', or comply with the expectation, or (even better) assume the responsibility. And, we need to understand that our cooperation is essential to building a productive learning environment.

"I have experienced many situations in which the rules seemed bureaucratic and not purposeful. Just this morning, I called a department store to inquire about an item that I had ordered by phone (to save time). It has not arrived after 4 weeks, although I was told at the time of the order that it would take 2-3 weeks. I was told this morning that the 'rule' is that it will not be reordered until 6 weeks from the time of the order, and if it is reordered, it will definitely come in 2 weeks. . . . I got the feeling that the person I spoke to was more concerned (and satisfied!) with following the rules than in making customers happy! Why is she there in the first place?" - Marley C.

Appendix A
Treat Yourself

*"When you recover or discover something that nour-
ishes your soul and brings joy, care enough about
yourself to make room for it in your life."*
                                        -- Jean Shinoda Bolen

Stop punishing yourself. Stop being so critical, so intolerant. Lighten up. It's time to start treating yourself well, and one of the best strategies for doing so is to give yourself treats -- early and often.

Authors Gillian Butler and Tony Hope articulate this strategy in their book *Managing Your Mind**, insisting that "the ability to give yourself treats and rewards is one of the basic strategies for improving mental fitness. . . . The wonderful thing about treats is that they can give pleasure well beyond what would seem possible. The secret is to choose the right treats for you. Once we are grown-up, life can become so full of chores, both at home and at work, that it is easy to get bogged down in routine and forget pleasure. . . . It is when life's problems are getting on top of you that it becomes particularly important to reward yourself . . . ."

Butler and Hope explain that giving yourself treats " . . . is a skill that needs to be developed. The first step is *to give yourself permission to have treats.* Treats bring pleasure, and pleasure is worth having purely because it makes you feel good. But treating yourself will also enable you to accomplish more, and enable you to change in ways that are right for you. *Giving yourself treats is the right way to treat yourself."*

---

*Information in this appendix is drawn from Butler & Hope's book: "Managing Your Mind: The Mental Fitness Guide," published by Oxford University Press. Permission to reprint was granted by United Agents, on the authors' behalf.

Our authors prescribe a 3-step system for "treating" ourselves:

Step 1: Pick the Treats that Work for You;
Step 2: Make Your System Work to Your Advantage; and
Step 3: Avoid the Punishment Trap.

So, without delay, why not treat yourself to Butler and Hope's vision. It's guaranteed to bring pleasure into your life.

Step 1 -- Pick the Treats that Work For You

Butler and Hope explain: "Think about things that you enjoy, that give you pleasure, that make you laugh, or help you to relax. Think of small things like spending an extra few minutes over breakfast, and big things like taking a holiday. Think of things you could buy now or save up for and get later; things that you could do for yourself and things you could say to yourself; things involving others and things for yourself alone. Try and make a list of 20 things. The longer the list the better."

Step 2 -- Make Your Treat System Work To Your Advantage

Butler and Hope's formula is six-fold:

"1. Get the timing right. Treats work best when they come quickly after the specific goal. Immediately after forcing yourself to sort out the unpaid bills, give yourself a treat. If you treat yourself first the bills will be even harder to face, and if you delay the treat when you have paid the bills, the connection between the two will be lost.

"2. Treat yourself often. Everyone would benefit from a daily treat: small pleasures make life easier and more pleasurable. But make sure that you do not use treats which fail to satisfy. If rewards like shopping or having another cigarette, drink or doughnut only perpetuate the search for pleasure, or make you feel better or less lonely only briefly, they may be the wrong kinds of treat for you.

"3. Saving up and cashing in. You may want to save up for a big treat like a new piece of sports equipment, or an item of clothing, or a day's outing. If so, give yourself tokens toward what you want. Decide how many it is worth (for example, you could go out for a meal when you have earned 20 "tokens") and use a tick in your diary as the marker of when you have earned a token. As you

Some Ideas for Treats & Rewards

Butler & Hope offer a host of treats and rewards for every style. Take a look and find one or two that nourish your soul.

♦ "Things to eat or drink, for example: having a chocolate biscuit, a glass of wine, your favorite meal, a cup of tea;

♦ "Activities, for example: taking a walk, watching TV or a video, planning an outing, enjoying a hobby, doing a puzzle or the crossword, playing bridge, poker, or your favorite game of cards with friends, gardening, going to a restaurant for dinner;

♦ "Relaxations, for example: listening to music, taking a long bath, calling a friend, reading a novel or magazine, sitting by the fire;

♦ "Treats, for example: buying a bunch of flowers or a bar of scented soap, planning a trip to the theater, buying a new piece of clothing, getting up late;

♦ "Time, for example: 10 minutes on your own, a mid-morning break, a proper lunch hour, time to think, a weekend break, a holiday;

♦ "Exercise, for example: joining the local gym, taking an exercise class, going for a swim, walking the dog;

♦ "Self-talk, for example: 'I'm doing fine,' 'I'm really pleased with . . . ,' 'Well done,' 'You can make it,' 'You deserve a break';

♦ "Setting limits, for example: number of chores, bedtime, a time to stop work, demands made by others;

♦ "Other people, for example: chatting by phone with or visiting a friend or relative, having a long lunch with an old friend."

collect more ticks, you can see how well you are doing.

"4. Give yourself variety. You might get bored with the same treat just as with anything else, and then it loses its power to encourage. Like a diet of pure chocolate, it could lose its appeal entirely. So update your treat system from time to time, remembering that different things feel like treats at different times. Going for a long walk may be your idea of fun in the summer, but in the winter you might prefer to watch TV. You may not value peace and quiet as much at 25 (when being on your own might feel more like a punishment than a reward) as you do at 35, when the thought of a few moments to yourself can feel like pure luxury. Or the challenge that you might enjoy at 50 (traveling on your own) may feel overwhelming at 19.

"5. Give yourself a break. Not doing one of the chores when you are worn out can feel good even though you know you will have to do it later. Allow yourself such breaks, and remember that a change can be as good as a rest if you need one badly. It might feel better to swap chores with someone else from time to time.

"6. Turn routine pleasures into effective rewards. Leaving all the things you hate doing to the last is like creating a quagmire to struggle through later -- probably when your energy and enthusiasm are at a low ebb. For example, if you have a coffee break every morning, this will feel more enjoyable, and work better as a reward if you do one hateful task before it rather than after."

Step 3 -- Avoid the Punishment Trap

Finally, Butler and Hope teach us how to avoid the punishment trap: "Do not make a virtue out of being a martyr. Do not fall into the trap of serving other people's needs so much at the expense of your own that you carry the sacrifice too far. Overburdening yourself 'for the sake of others,' treating yourself unfairly, makes others feel guilty and can become an undeclared way of punishing them. Saying, 'don't worry, I can manage' when you really mean quite the opposite punishes both you and others. In the long run everyone is worse off, and you may be building up resentment within yourself that will eventually burst out in anger, or push in on you as depression. Beating your head against a brick wall is another version of the same thing. It feels good when you stop beating yourself, but if this is your only reward for tackling the brick wall, then persisting in punishing yourself is pointless."

Appendix B

Learning to Pause

*"The secret of your future is hidden
in your daily routine."*
-- Mike Murdock

How many times a day do you shift gears? How many times a day do you transition from one activity to another?

Is is 50? 100? 200? Now imagine if you learned to pause, truly pause, during each of these transitional moments.

Author Hugh Prather* instructs us to pause during life's "natural stopping points" -- moments when our mind shifts its attention from one activity to the next. Explains Prather:

> *"There are many times -- far more than are recognized at first -- when we get so caught up in the day's problems and events that only by pausing and intentionally stilling our thoughts will our awareness expand enough to take in all the ways we are limiting our options. To solve life's little problems, as well as most of the big ones, the first experience we need is to see what happens when the bumping stops."*

Prather's cautionary note:

> *"Many people think they already know the benefits of pausing, but unless this practice has become as second nature as breathing, they have not yet enjoyed the benefits sufficiently."*

---

* Prather is author of "How to Live in the World and Still Be Happy."

Here then is Prather's two-step approach to pausing:

Step 1 is to notice that the day comes in segments; and Step 2 is to pause (just a moment or two), during what these "transitional periods." Prather eloquently explains:

> *"Notice that the day comes in segments, with little beginnings and endings to each. Also notice that the mind refocuses with each change of bodily activity. This is true whether or not we finish a task. Our sense of completion varies with our sense of expectation. However thorough or incomplete we assess our efforts to be, the day still proceeds as a chain of events rather than as a continuous stream. Our mind makes a brief transition or adjustment in going from one activity to another, from sleep ending to waking up, from making the bed to getting dressed, from getting dressed to eating breakfast, and so forth. Notice, too, that there is a natural stopping point during this instant when the mind is shifting gears. It is 'natural' because if done happily it facilitates and smoothes this shift as well as provides many other pleasant and more lasting benefits.*

> *"To take advantage of these transitional periods, all that's necessary is to notice them, then pause and calm the mind for a few seconds. Usually it's easier to settle the mind when the body is still. We can quietly stand where we are, or perhaps sit a moment with our eyes closed. Only an instant or two is needed.*

> *"We want a sense of the mind slowing and settling down, somewhat like coming to a stop at an intersection and allowing the car's engine to idle for a moment. We let the mind drift easily and happily. We avoid pursuing any one thought. Some individuals like to listen peacefully to the sounds around them. Others prefer to become aware of their breathing. Some like to repeat calming words such as 'My mind is quiet. I am still now.' Any way of pausing is fine, provided it doesn't add a sense of burden or duty."*

Material in Appendix B is excerpted from the book HOW TO LIVE IN THE WORLD AND STILL BE HAPPY © 2002 Hugh Prather with permission from Red Wheel/Weiser, LLC Newburyport, MA and San Francisco, CA www.redwheelweiser.com.

Appendix C
Too Many Bad Habits?
Start Shoveling

"The more deeply the path is etched,
the more it is used, and the more
it is used, the more deeply it is etched."
-- Jo Coudert

Imagine that your habits (good or bad) are like holes in the earth. Each time that a new habit is created, a new hole begins to grow. And as years pass, and more and more ground is unearthed, the bottom of the hole is nearly impossible to see.

We acquire habits for a panoply of reasons -- to make friends (e.g., smoking), reduce anxiety (e.g., drinking), bring comfort (e.g., over-eating), and satisfy egos (e.g., talking endlessly about ourselves). Sometimes our habits are physical (e.g., picking our nails), and sometimes they're more cerebral (e.g., judging our friends). But no matter the source, habits are difficult to change.

That's why you'll need some special equipment (perhaps a shovel and a new pair of gloves). If habits are like holes in the ground, the best way to change them is to start pitching fresh dirt into the hole. Keep in mind, of course, that it might take a while to fill up the hole. But until you've filled it completely, with enough fresh earth to smooth things over, the habit will live on.

For the most part, we have control over how long our habits persist; after all, we can choose to start pitching fresh dirt. There are times, of course, when natural forces will add or detract -- a wind storm might assist us, a strong rain might slow our flight. But regardless of outside forces, we are largely in control. It's simply a matter of how often we decide to take out the shovel.

At times, we consciously decide when to fill the hole (i.e., eliminate bad habits) and when to dig (i.e., create new ones). But, more often than not, the holes in our lives simply appear, without a great deal of forethought or intent.

Why not combine the two?

Indeed, experts maintain that the best way to arrest an old habit is to replace it with a new one. Explains Dr. Pat Hudson, author and psychotherapist: "Substitute something that you will feel good about for the old habit. For example if the old habit was biting your nails, every time you start towards your mouth with your hand, caress your nails with your thumb. With smoking you might consult your doctor for nicorettes gum or a patch to help you through quitting. After a few days the nicotine addiction is usually gone and the only thing you must deal with then is all the associations you had with the habit."

Linking new habits to old ones certainly seems efficient -- after all, when we start digging the dirt for our new habit, we can use this same earth to fill in our old one. But life doesn't always present such convenient opportunities, which is why the bulk of the self-help literature focuses on getting rid of our bad habits.

Creating new habits, of course, can be a disappointing enterprise, which is why you'll enjoy this playful post by Leo Babauta of zenhabits.net who tells us what *not* to do when creating new habits.

How to Fail at Habits, by Leo Babauta:

"I failed at creating new habits repeatedly. Here's what I did, and what most people also do:

"1.Take on multiple habits at once. We have lots of things we want to change, so we try to change them all at once. Of course, this spreads our focus and energy thin, so that we can't give our entire focus to any one habit. Habits are hard to change, and spreading yourself thin is a good way to make sure you fail.

"2. Bite off more than you can chew. Whether you do one habit or many at a time, try to do as much with each habit as possible, so that it takes up a lot of energy and seems really hard. Don't run for 5 minutes, try doing 30. That way it'll be a big chunk of your day that will get pushed to tomorrow when other urgent things come up, it will take a lot of your physical and mental energy, and it'll be something you dread doing because it's so difficult. Don't meditate for 5 minutes, meditate for

60. Do 90 minutes of yoga. Change your entire diet all at once. These are excellent ways to fail.

"**3. Tackle habits you don't enjoy.** *Because habits should be something you do for moral reasons — they're good for you! And so it doesn't matter if you hate them, and if you dread doing them after awhile, because you're going to be disciplined. That works extremely seldomly, so it's a great strategy.*

"**4. Keep it a secret.** *Don't tell anyone you're changing your habit. That way, if you mess up, it won't be embarrassing. This means that you secretly think you're going to mess up, which is another excellent way to fail.*

"**5. Jump right into it.** *Decide today to start running, and just do it! This way you are treating it as if it's nothing, and not a big commitment. You don't plan for obstacles, don't set up a support system, don't give yourself rewards, and treat the habit change as lightly as you do putting on your socks. And when you quit doing the habit, it will be no problem either.*

"**6. Don't worry about how others have succeeded.** *Why read the success stories of other people? You know better than them. You can do it without learning from them. That's what I used to think, at least.*

"**7. Don't motivate yourself.** *You don't need motivation if you have discipline. Discipline is something you have or don't have, but motivation is something you can actually do.*

"**8. Give yourself plenty of opportunities to give up.** *Trying to eat healthy? Have your cupboards and fridge filled with junk food, and have it surround you at work, and go to restaurants filled with fried foods and sugary sweets. You'll definitely have the discipline to ignore those.*

"*The eight steps above are a sure-fire recipe for habit failure, and I recommend you try all of them if you're looking to fail. Of course, if you're looking to succeed, you might want to avoid them and possibly try the opposite.*"

Appendix D

Tip for Creating New Habits:

Recruit Strong Partners

Leo Babauta of zenhabits.net offers this unique tip for creating new habits: find strong partners. Explains Babauta, in this informative web post:

"If you've struggled with habit change yourself, recruit some help.

"But who do you ask? And how do you find the right partners in crime? Unfortunately, not just anyone is a good fit. Picking the right person that will complement you is just as important as picking someone at all.

"Fair warning: Friends and relatives do not always make the best accountability partners.

"Through plenty of trial and error, I've found a few characteristics that I look for in someone I'm about to partner with to make an important life change. Perhaps they'll help you find a good fit, too.

  • "They're a little ahead of you, but not too far ahead. In a good accountability partnership, one person is usually at least a little bit further beyond the other. Though you're both helping each other, one person stands out as the more likely mentor. Otherwise, it's the blind leading the blind. And you don't want your partner to be too far ahead of you, or the relationship is unbalanced and feels awkward.

  • "They're a little bit competitive. You probably don't want someone who's looking to stick it to you every chance they get, but you'll get a lot further a lot faster if your accountability partner isn't satisfied with self defeat and is willing to actually hold you accountable.

  • "They have similar goals to you. You don't have to be working on the exact same thing to work well with a partner — it can be great to work together on separate projects — but there should be an obvious overlap of your big goals. There needs to be something that ties you two together beyond just "wanting to change something.

• "They're focused. If you agree to meet for 10 minutes each day, but never seem to get anywhere because your meetings are unfocused, first look at yourself. Are you dragging things off course on a regular basis? If not, then it's probably time to find a more focused partner.

• "They're supportive when you need it. This goes back to competitiveness. You want your partner to push you and hold you accountable — that's what they're there for — but a good one also has your best interest at heart and knows when you need a little lift instead of a scolding.

• "They show commitment. The truth is that you can usually tell if a partnership like this is going to work within a week. If your accountability partner can't even get it together at the very beginning when excitement is running high, that's a pretty good indication they're not committed to change. Best to get out. This doesn't make them a bad person, but it probably makes them a bad partner for now.

"If you've ever struggled with making an important habit change in your life, then I challenge you to step out of your comfort zone and ask for help. If you're like me, it could turn everything around.

"What do you want to change? Who can help?"

Appendix E
How Good a Listener Are You?

"No one ever listened
themselves out of a job."
-- Calvin Coolidge

What kind of listener are you? On a scale of 1-10, how would be rate yourself as a listener (10 is the highest)?

When you have a few minutes, try the accompanying 8-part "Listening Self Assessment." You just might be surprised at the result.

Four levels
The Center for Organizational and Personal Excellence maintains that we generally listen at one of four levels:

> **1. Ignoring** – not really listening at all;

> **2. Pretending** – not listening, but providing verbal/non-verbal cues;

> **3. Selective/Attentive Listening** – listening only to what one "wants" to hear; and

> **4. Empathetic Listening** – listening with intent to understand.

And when it comes to empathetic listening, the Center describes 4 stages:

Stage 1 – Mimicking
> *TEAM LEADER: "I've had it! This performance management process is for the birds!"*
> *MANAGER: "You've had it. You think that the performance management process is for the birds."*

Stage 2 – Rephrasing

TEAM LEADER: *"I've had it! This performance management process is for the birds!*

MANAGER: *"You don't want to deal with the performance management process anymore."*

Stage 3 – Reflecting

TEAM LEADER: *"I've had it! This performance management process is for the birds!"*

MANAGER: *"You're really frustrated with the performance management process."*

Stage 4 – Rephrasing & Reflecting

TEAM LEADER: *"I've had it! This performance management process is for the birds!"*

MANAGER: *"You're really frustrated with the performance management process."*

TEAM LEADER: *(thinks: "That's right, that's how I feel") "I sure am. It's totally impractical."*

MANAGER: *"You feel that there is no value in the performance management process."*

TEAM LEADER: *(thinks: let me think, is that what I mean?) "Well . . . I just don't understand how we can do our day to day job AND also the performance management process."*

MANAGER: *"You're not sure that our performance management process is practical."*

TEAM LEADER: *(thinks: well . . .) "Well, I guess we have to use some process to establish objectives and measure and monitor progress. But, how do we find the time to apply the performance objectives, performance factors and development plan to each of our staff and still accomplish our work as a team leader?"*

MANAGER: *"How about if we set up a meeting with several colleagues and representatives from the Human Resources Department to discuss how we can more effectively implement the performance management process with our staff?"*

Challenge: No I's

In their module on building listening skills ("Listening is a Voluntary Act,") the Center for Organizational and Personal Excellence (COPE) offers this challenge. Try it out with a close friend, and see what happens:

> For two minutes, have a conversation with another person without using the word "I", or the words me, she, he or it. I've tried it . . . quite the challenge!

Listening time
"Approximately 45% of all time spent commu-nicating involves listening; next comes speaking with 30%, reading with 16% and writing with 9%." -- COPE

Listening vs. Hearing
"Hearing is a physical act,
Listening is an emotional act."
-- COPE

Listen = Silent
How about this oddity . . . if you take the letters in the word LISTEN and rearrange them, you come up with the word SILENT. What are the chances?

Listening: Self Assessment*

If you are serious about improving your listening skills, try this 8-part listening self-assessment (~4-6 minutes to fill out). Better yet, ask some clients, or co-workers (or friends) to complete this assessment for you.

To complete the survey: 1 = needs much improvement, 5 = a strength

1. Mechanics:

1 2 3 4 5 I seat myself in a way that encourages listening.

1 2 3 4 5 I do not allow the telephone to interfere with listening.

1 2 3 4 5 I know I can think faster than clients speak. I use this time to find patterns in my client's words.

1 2 3 4 5 I make brief notes of what I want to say before the meeting so I can concentrate on what my client is saying.

1 2 3 4 5 I make brief notes during the meeting of how I want to respond so I can keep my mind on my client's words.

2. Listening with my eyes:

1 2 3 4 5 I make eye contact early.

1 2 3 4 5 I maintain an appropriate level of eye contact.

1 2 3 4 5 I am conscious of cultural differences in non-verbal behavior, particularly eye contact.

1 2 3 4 5 I am conscious of my client's non-verbal behaviors.

1 2 3 4 5 I use my client's non-verbal clues to help me assess appropriate replies to clients.

3. Appropriate silence:

1 2 3 4 5 I give my clients time to complete their thoughts.

1 2 3 4 5 I give my clients "air time."

1 2 3 4 5 I am conscious of silence periods.

1 2 3 4 5 I can remain silent to help clients state deeper thoughts and feelings.

4. Asking good questions:

1 2 3 4 5 I know how to use questions to show I am listening.

1 2 3 4 5 I know how to use questions to help a client "talk through" an issue.

1 2 3 4 5 I am aware of and know when to use a range of questions from closed-ended to open-ended.

1 2 3 4 5 I formulate a questioning strategy rather than asking whatever pops into my head.

1 2 3 4 5 I understand that I can ask questions which keep me in my "comfort zone."

1 2 3 4 5 I can use questions to help clients surface objections or resistance to my ideas.

(continued)

* reproduced with permission from Powerful Professionals by Murray Hiebert

5. Actively listening to content:

1 2 3 4 5 I consciously use restatement, summarizing, and paraphrasing before I give my point of view.

1 2 3 4 5 I consciously ask for clarification if I do not understand my client.

1 2 3 4 5 I am aware of the difference between an observation and evaluation.

1 2 3 4 5 I am able to name problems in a way that does not make them personal.

1 2 3 4 5 I can ask for a summary.

1 2 3 4 5 I am aware of the difference between listening for content and listening for process.

6. Listening for process:

1 2 3 4 5 I understand when to respond to process rather than content.

1 2 3 4 5 I have a repertoire of process tools for suggesting more powerful ways for dealing with consulting situations.

1 2 3 4 5 I am able to meta-communicate, that is, talk about what we are talking about.

1 2 3 4 5 I understand the power of framing issues.

1 2 3 4 5 I can help clients reframe when appropriate.

7. Listening for emotions:

1 2 3 4 5 I can "hear" the emotion in my client's words, voice, tone, and other non-verbals.

1 2 3 4 5 I can listen by reflecting the emotion I hear.

1 2 3 4 5 I know when it is appropriate to make a listening response to my client's emotion.

1 2 3 4 5 I know I cannot fix emotions, I can only help clients express them.

1 2 3 4 5 I do not suppress conflict or anger by changing the subject.

8. Listening as a whole:

1 2 3 4 5 I often ask for feedback on my listening skills.

1 2 3 4 5 I understand my "comfort zone" for dealing with ambiguity and conflict.

1 2 3 4 5 I understand that all behavior makes sense in my client's frame of reference.

1 2 3 4 5 I use a wide range of listening skills.

1 2 3 4 5 I can listen to others.

1 2 3 4 5 I am considered an effective listener by others.

> **A Confidant**
> *"Let others confide in you. It may not help you, but it surely will help them."*
>
> *-- Roger G. Imhoff*

Appendix F
The Human Translator

*"When we talk about understanding, surely it takes
place only when the mind listens completely -- the
mind being your heart, your nerves, your ears --
when you give your whole attention to it."*
                            -- Jiddu Krishnamurti

Let's create a new dictionary. Not to replace Webster's, mind you, just to supplement it. Our proposed new dictionary would take a person's literal words and translate them into their real meaning. Perhaps we'll call it *"The Human Translator."*

So when a spouse in the passenger seat blurts out:

"Why didn't you check the directions before we started?"

. . . a quick thumb-through *The Human Translator* would reveal that the passenger is a touch anxious about being late and the embarrassment that it might cause.

And when a child from the back seat repeatedly asks:

"Are we there yet?"

. . . *The Human Translator* would reveal that the child has little with which to keep their mind busy, plus a limited vocabulary with which to engage an adult in conversation.

When a teenager suddenly offers:

"I hate going on family vacations."

. . . *The Human Translator* would inform us that the teenager simply misses her friends or is momentarily bored.

If I could locate a copy of this new dictionary I would waste no time looking up two of my favorite words: "always" and "never." These are two words that trigger my emotional system, as in:

*"You **never** let me sleep over her house."*

*"You **always** treat me like a child."*

*"You **never** let me go to the concerts at night."*

*"I **always** have to do the recycling by myself."*

Too often, the response that leaps from my lips is: "Always! What are you talking about? Why just last week . . . " But then I realize that I'm reacting to the words instead of their meaning, and I quickly understand (sometimes, not quickly enough) that my literal rendering is misplaced.

It's times like these when I need to flip through my personal copy of *The Human Translator.* If I did, it would explain why people use words like "never" and "always" -- presumably to strengthen their position, to get what they want. And it might even help me understand why I *always* get flustered when I hear those trigger words.

So the next time you're in a bookstore, stop by the information desk and ask for a copy of *The Human Translator.* If the information clerk looks puzzled, explain that it's a book that takes the literal words that people speak and translates them into their actual meaning, devoid of anger and irritation, harm and criticism.

If they *still* can't find it, take out a pen and pencil and start writing your own. It just might become the most valuable book that you own.

Appendix G
Will You Please Just Listen?

A poem, author unknown:

"When I ask you to listen
and you start giving advice,
you have not done what I have asked;

"When I ask you to listen
and you begin to tell me
why I shouldn't feel the way I do,
you are trampling on my feelings;

"When I ask you to listen
and you feel you have to do something
to solve my problem,
you have failed me, strange as that may seem.

"Listen! All I asked was that you listen,
not talk to or do -- just hear me.

"When you do something for me
that I can and need to do for myself,
you contribute to my fear and inadequacy.

"But when you accept the way I feel,
no matter how irrational,
then I don't need to spend time and energy
trying to defend myself or convince you,
and I can focus on figuring out why I feel the way I feel
and what to do about it.
And when I do that, I don't need advice,
just support, trust and encouragement.

"So please listen and just hear me.
And if you yourself want or need to talk,
wait a minute and I will listen to you."

Appendix H
Learning How to Take Risks

Looking for a job? The experts at Wordscapes (a resume service) offer this candid advice for job seekers:

"If you're the type of person who can't make a move without being certain of the outcome, you're going to be very uncomfortable in a period of transition. It's time to build some risk-taking confidence.

"**Calculate**. Be sure you realize the consequences. Never risk more than you are willing to lose.

"**Minimize**. Reduce your chance of loss by doing research, building support and getting as much control as possible over the outcome.

> "Ask yourself:
> "What could go wrong?
> "What are the chances of that happening?
> "How can I lessen the risk?
> "If I don't take the risk, what would I lose?
> "Can I break the risk down into steps or smaller risks that I can take one at a time?

"**Practice**. Take small risks first to build up your confidence.

"**Try something new**. Talk to people you don't know. Go places you haven't been before - even a different store - or take a new route to work. Changing your routine can add creativity to your life.

"**Learn from setbacks**. Look at risks that fail as opportunities to learn.

"Learn what you don't like from different experiences. It's never a waste of time to have experienced something you found unpleasant. Knowing what you don't like is as important as knowing what you do like."

Appendix I

On the Physics
of Rocks

*"If you want to make good use of your time,
you've got to know what's most important
and then give it all you've got."*
-- Lee Iacocca

*This compelling tale, circulated via the Internet for
years, makes clear an eternal truth -- that unless we set
our priorities, and stick to them, we'll be swept along on
the tide of daily crises. Listen then, to how an "expert in
time management" brings his students to life.*

One day an expert in time management was speaking to a group of business students and, to drive home a point, used an illustration those students will never forget.

As he stood in front of the group of high powered over-achievers he said, "Okay, time for a quiz." Then he pulled out a one-gallon, wide-mouthed Mason jar and set it on the table in front of him. He then produced about a dozen fist-sized rocks and carefully placed them, one at a time, into the jar. When the jar was filled to the top and no more rocks would fit inside, he asked, "Is this jar full?"

Everyone in the class said, "Yes," to which he asked, "Really?" He reached under the table and pulled out a bucket of gravel. Then he dumped some gravel in and shook the jar, causing pieces of gravel to work themselves down into the space between the big rocks.

Then he asked the group once more, "Is the jar full?" By this time the class was on to him. "Probably not," one of them answered.

"Good!" he replied. He reached under the table and brought out a bucket of sand. He started dumping the sand in the jar, and it went into all of the spaces left between the rocks and the gravel. Once more he asked the question, "Is this jar full?" "No!" the class shouted. Once again he said, "Good."

He grabbed a pitcher of water and began to pour it in, filling the jar to the brim. Then he looked at the class and asked, "What is the point of this illustration?" One eager beaver raised his hand and said, "The point is, no matter how full your schedule is, if you try really hard you can always fit some more things in it!"

"No," the speaker replied, "that's not the point. The truth this illustration teaches us is: If you don't put the big rocks in first, you'll never get them in at all."

What are the "big rocks" in your life? Your children? Your loved ones? Your education? Your dreams? A worthy cause? Teaching or mentoring others? Doing things that you love? Time for yourself? Your health? Your significant other?

Remember to put these big rocks in first or you'll never get them in at all.

If you sweat the little stuff (the gravel, the sand) then you'll fill your life with little things you worry about that don't really matter, and you'll never have the real quality time you need to spend on the big, important stuff (the big rocks).

So, tonight, when you're reflecting on this short story, ask yourself: What are the "big rocks" in my life? Put those in first.

Just a Tool

"Goals are a means to an end, not the ultimate purpose of our lives. They are simply a tool to concentrate our focus and move us in a direction. The only reason we really pursue goals is to cause ourselves to expand and grow. Achieving goals by themselves will never make us happy in the long term; it's who you become, as you overcome the obstacles necessary to achieve your goals, that can give you the deepest and most long-lasting sense of fulfillment." -- Anthony Robbins

Appendix J
How Many Bumps Have You Had Today?
The Theory of Six Bumps

"We can't have a crisis tomorrow.
My schedule is already full."
-- Henry Kissinger

Why do we expect so much?

Why do we expect the ATMs to work every time? Why do we expect our close friend to respond in a timely fashion? Why do we expect light traffic on Saturday morning? Why do we expect our children to act in a certain manner? Why do we expect that today will proceed with no interruptions, no mis-steps, no bumps?

These days, I try to live by the "Theory of Six Bumps." It's a simple premise: each day will surprise us with six "bumps," that is, events that we could never have anticipated, but must deal with nonetheless. The dog gets sick and does her business on the carpet (bump #1) . . . a friend desperately needs a ride to drop off his car (bump #2) . . . on our way to the office, we realize that we forgot one critical piece for the afternoon meeting (bump #3).

If we're lucky, most of our bumps will be insignificant, but every now and then, some bumps turn into hills, others into mountains. During moments like these, we're forced to spend more time climbing, and less time cruising.

If you're lucky, of course, you'll only have six a day. But rest assured, they'll arrive -- tomorrow, and the next day, and the day after that.

Some time ago I shared the "Theory of Six Bumps" with my sister. It was less than 48 hours later when she called and reported, "Well, I've already had my six bumps today." The remarkable news was that she was calling at 10:30am (as best as I can recollect, three of the bumps involved a parking ticket, a broken coffee pot and a computer glitch, a tough trio if you asked me).

In practice, the "Theory of Six Bumps" can be an emotional life saver because it turns the unexpected . . . into the expected. Rather than anticipating a day free of mishaps (hope springs eternal), anticipate a day full of mishaps; then, when they arrive, you're all set! Granted, you still might not be thrilled when they arrive, but at least you'll be prepared, emotionally.

Some days, I give voice to my bumps. Rushing to a morning meeting, I spot a traffic jam up ahead. Inside I'm thinking: "Bump #1". Hours later, on the checkout line I discover that I don't have my credit card (bump #2) because I gave it to my daughter (an altogether different kind of bump). Once home, I realize that I've neglected to shut off the outside water valve and discover that the water line has burst (bump #3, no, that's more like a hill).

Most major bumps, of course, have to do with health -- when disease strikes, backs inflame, knee cartilage tears. These are the days when we're forced to climb a little longer, a little faster.

An interesting bump arrived some weeks ago, at 9:25am on a Saturday morning. While at home, finishing up breakfast, Roe and I heard a strange noise emanating from the air vent. Within minutes we realized that an animal was somehow trapped in the duct system and suddenly my frustration level began to soar. It was clear, *this* Saturday was about to disappear. Suddenly, I smiled to myself and said aloud: "Ahhhh, bump #1." Six hours later, the problem was resolved. And while frustration was still a part of the profile, the self-recognition helped immensely.

Might a bump-free day lie in your future? Not a chance. So just sit back and relax - and count 'em if you wish. But know this: bumps will arrive again tomorrow . . . and the day after that.

Embrace reality. It's a heckuva lot less frustrating.

Appendix K

Are You a Light Switch or a Dimmer?

You may think of yourself as a light switch, but I assure you: you're really a dimmer.

When the Light Switch asks: Are you an introvert or an extrovert?, the Dimmer responds: I'm a touch of each.

And when the Light Switch asks: Are you fun-loving or serious?, the Dimmer responds: I'm a touch of each.

Throughout our lives we typecast others AND ourselves -- introvert or extrovert, attractive or plain, conservative or liberal, fun-loving or serious, powerful or frail, diligent or lazy, adventurous or timorous. These labels, of course, serve us poorly, because, at times, we're both introverted and extroverted, attractive and plain, conservative and liberal -- just rarely at the same time.

The crime -- and I truly believe it to be a crime -- is how these personality labels shape our lives and our decisions. It doesn't have to be that way. If we learn to view our personality along a continuum -- from introvert to extrovert, from fun-loving to serious, from firm to flexible, and back again -- we would be more free to evolve new traits, new human characteristics. We wouldn't feel as "locked in" to our current personality.

The challenge, of course, is to "unlock" our personality, to allow each of our traits to freely flow along the continuum (from powerful to frail, from adventurous to timorous, then back again), to allow every part of our personality to be malleable and flexible. To unlock our personality is to free ourselves of a heavy weight, the weight of past decisions and historical labels. A quick mental review of your actions in the past week will reveal what you know intellectually -- that you're neither "diligent" nor "lazy" all the time; instead you blend the two, as circumstances dictate.

It may be appealing to view all personality traits as controlled by a dimmer, instead of a light switch. After all, a dimmer allows us to to control, to freely adjust. A light switch does nothing of the sort -- it's only on or off.

If we take a moment to look at any single personality trait (honesty, courage, generosity, steadfastness, ability to listen), it's easy to recognize that you're not "either-or." Sadly, members of society long to lock us in, and at times that pressure is merciless. But if we are to grow our past decisions ("I thought you didn't like to . . ." or "I never enjoy movies that . . . "), we must recognize that we're free to flow up and down the continuum, whenever desired.

The key question, of course, becomes "How flexible are you?" And the underlying point is steadfast -- human traits exist on a continuum; they're neither stagnant nor fixed. They flow, and evolve, much as we do as human beings.

So remember to think of yourself as a dimmer, and allow yourself to turn it up, or turn it down, based on the occasion.

Appendix L

"We Have Very High Expectations of Our Students"

-- Middle School Principal, in a memo to parents

Is that a good thing? And, when the principal uses these words, does he mean "goals" or "expectations?"

The English language offers a surfeit of words to describe the pursuit of human achievement. But in exploring the distinction of words that are commonly intermingled, confusion (not clarity) reigns.

Let's take a look at what we *create*. Customarily, human beings create goals, plans, objectives, targets and benchmarks (and use these to create "personal mission" and/or "personal vision" statements). We create them, they don't just appear. And in *creating* these items (I call these "conscious creations"), we do so with a sense of control, a sense that we have choices that we alone can make. Well, sort of.

Hidden behind the conscious mask are our "subconscious" counterparts -- those parts of our personality that are hidden from view but which nonetheless play a critical role in our ability to achieve and our ability to enjoy. And similar to "expectations," we don't create them; instead, they simply evolve. We're talking, of course, about our attitudes, values, principles, opinions and expectations. We don't consciously create them yet their existence is as vital to the goal-setting process as our conscious creations (this calls to mind the fifth element in the goal-setting process -- the importance of aligning one's goal with one's values).

There are times, of course, when it's difficult to tell the difference between goals and expectations ("we have very high expectations for our students"), when it's hard, if not impossible, to delineate between values and objectives ("we wish to insure that our children grow up with a sense of respect and fairness"). But the distinctions are meaningful and guide our decisions -- more than we might care to admit.

If you choose to think about the differences between "conscious" and "subconscious" creations, you'll immediately vault yourself into an arena where few travel. But for those who venture, the trip is extraordinary.

About the Author

Author Steve Ferber never stops exploring. Over a 30-year business career as journalistic and entrepreneur, Mr. Ferber has started six companies and a dozen publications, and currently authors a blog called "Unconventional Wisdom" (http://riveresque.blogspot.com/). He has three passions in life -- his family, education and psychology, and this book is devoted to his lifelong interest in personal growth.

His business career began in 1974 at Fairchild Publications in New York City -- five years later he joined two colleagues to start Inside Washington Publishers, a newsletter publishing company which tracks key policy decisions by the federal government. From a three-person staff, the company now employs more than 50 reporters and publishes more than two dozen newsletters and online services. Through the 1980s, Steve was part of a team that launched Inside the White House, Inside EPA, Inside the Pentagon, Inside U.S. Trade, and a dozen related newsletters in the fields of defense, energy and the environment.

He sold his interest in the publishing firm in 1991 and began working as a full-time volunteer in the Fairfax County, VA school system (the 12th largest in the nation) -- mentoring, coaching, teaching, developing curriculum and initiating a host of volunteer programs (at the high school level, he teamed with the principal to teach a course titled "What's Worth Knowing?"). Over the last 15 years, Ferber has started four of his six companies -- an educational non-profit, a computer development firm, a publishing venture in the medical field, and a sports marketing company.

Steve and his wife Roe live in Charleston, SC, and their daughters Melyssa, Natalie and Olivia visit often (fortunately). Two sons (in-law) have joined the crew -- Dave and Trace, along with two grandchildren, Emery and Vincent. And dogs Wrigley and Shea (yes, both named by Olivia, as a baseball tribute) enjoy long walks on the beach.

CPSIA information can be obtained
at www.ICGtesting.com
Printed in the USA
BVHW01s1006020118
504196BV00003B/560/P